ABORIGINAL VOICES

'Guyamanda', lino print. Banduk Marika.
Previous Page: Paddy Roe.

ABORIGINAL VOICES

CONTEMPORARY ABORIGINAL ARTISTS, WRITERS AND PERFORMERS

COMPILED BY LIZ THOMPSON

For all those Voices of the past which were not heard.

ABORIGINAL VOICES

First published in Australasia in 1990 by
Simon & Schuster Australia
7 Grosvenor Place, Brookvale NSW 2100

A Paramount Communications Company
Sydney New York London Toronto Tokyo Singapore

©1990 Liz Thompson

All rights reserved. No part of this publication may be reproduced, stored in a retrieval system, or transmitted, in any form or by any means, electronic, mechanical, photocopying, recording or otherwise, without the prior permission of the publisher in writing.

National Library of Australia
Cataloguing in Publication data
Aboriginal voices: contemporary Aboriginal artists,
  writers and performers.

  Includes index.
  ISBN 0 7318 0165 2.

  [1]. Art, Australian – Aboriginal artists. [2]. Australian literature – Aboriginal authors. 3.   Entertainers – Australia. I. Thompson, Liz.

709.94

Designed by Jack Jagtenberg
Map artwork by Greg Campbell Design

Typeset in Australia by The Type Shop Pty. Limited
Printed in Hong Kong by South China Printing Company

Cover: 'Wrestling with White Spirit', Trevor Nickolls
       Background design – 'Armband (Parmitjiri)',
       Angelo Munkana, Tiwi Designs

The views expressed in the interviews in this book do not necessarily reflect those of the publisher.

FOREWORD

For just on 200 years Aboriginal voices were, for the most part silenced; and others wrote about Aborigines. The strangers' voices were either romantic with various versions of the "Noble Savage", or strident with denigration of the Blacks. This book, aptly titled *Aboriginal Voices*, is a collection of stories by Aboriginal people themselves. All of them are involved in the Arts, and all tell their own versions of the personal and collective experiences of Aborigines over the last 200 years.

The hallmark of those experiences has been destruction wrought by Anglo-Australians upon Aborigines: destruction of the very bodies of the people; destruction of their land, their languages, songs and dances; destruction of their identity. The Voices contained in these pages tell of these experiences, and of their individual efforts to triumph over those experiences.

There are people throughout Australian society who would continue the processes of destruction. One such process is the way in which they would define "real" Aboriginal culture as that of times past — a static view of culture. Unfortunately many of our people internalise this Anglo-Australian view. Often then, one hears that "we must go back to traditional culture". Some of the Voices in this book sound that call. But culture is about people living. It is a dynamic process.

Aboriginal culture is what Aboriginal people today are, with all our collective experiences. All of us of course carry our 40 000+ years of history within us. We lay on top of that our present experiences, and the outcomes are mixtures of pain, despair, bitterness, humour, optimism, resilience, anger, longing, a search for truth, a search for identity, a search for understanding — and these outcomes evoke parallel responses of laughter, tears or sheer bewilderment. And as our people live these experiences so they write, sing and dance.

All of this is "real" Aboriginal culture. It leaps out of real Aboriginal people, as every one of the Voices recorded in these pages tell. These stories, these histories, cannot — should not — be told once, put down, and forgotten.

All of these stories are within our lives now and for as long as our people shall endure. These histories will be told again and again, and some day these histories, captured in the paintings, the writings, the music and the dances of today, will become "traditional" Aboriginal culture.

This book is part of that important process.

Pat O'Shane A.M., LL.M.

CONTENTS

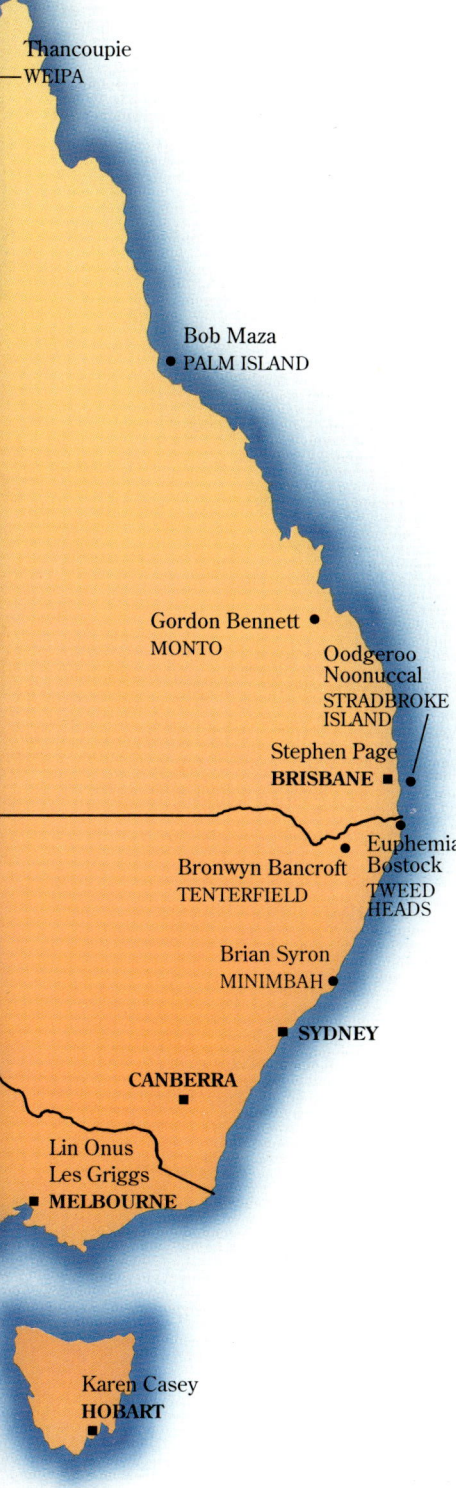

Introduction **8**

WESTERN AUSTRALIA

Jack Davis **12**
Glenyse Ward **18**
Jimmy Chi **24**
Paddy Roe **30**
Archie Weller **34**
Sally Morgan **39**
Peter Skipper **44**
Merrilee Lands **49**
Mudrooroo Narogin **55**
Pat Torres **60**
Richard Walley **65**

CENTRAL AUSTRALIA

Bede Tungutalum **72**
Geoffrey Gordon Lindsay **77**
Andrew Spencer Japaljarri **82**
Banduk Marika **86**
Doug Abbott **92**
Pansy Napangati **96**
Mandawuy Yunupingue **100**
Trevor Nickolls **104**
Delphine Geia **111**

EASTERN AUSTRALIA

Stephen Page **118**
Euphemia Bostock **123**
Lin Onus **128**
Bronwyn Bancroft **133**
Brian Syron **138**
Karen Casey **143**
Gordon Bennett **147**
Oodgeroo Noonuccal **154**
Bob Maza **159**
Thancoupie **164**
Les Griggs **168**

Acknowledgements **175**
Index **176**

INTRODUCTION

Contemporary Aboriginal arts are inextricably linked with the politics of being black in Australia. They examine Australian history and the Australian identity from an Aboriginal perspective — reviewing the historical "facts" which have been provided, re-selecting and re-presenting the information which has been made available to the public. I would say that almost all of the contemporary art, drama, music, theatre and literature produced by Aboriginal people draws on Aboriginal social context, Aboriginal experiences and Aboriginal history. It is, as a result, an entirely different view to that produced in the heroic European vein.

While the expressions of black Australia inevitably involve a condemnation of European colonisation, they also look to the future and to world and environmental issues.

Australia has been accused of suffering from a "cultural cringe", a feeling of cultural inadequacy, and of appropriating a European cultural identity. Much of the work of these artists examines the historical *production* of "Australia" and the silences enveloped to protect it. It seems feasible, as many of the artists who speak in this book would suggest, that until the history of the dispossession of the indigenous people of Australia is acknowledged, a uniquely Australian identity will not develop.

Contemporary Aboriginal arts constitute a strong component of a new kind of Aboriginal identity, while often drawing on more traditional influences. There are degrees of influence which are acceptable: direct appropriation is not. While many artists derive inspiration from tradition, many speak of the importance of evolution — establishing new forms, symbols and sounds to describe a new and current situation. Many artists suggest that through combining traditional influences with contemporary mediums and expressions, a more appropriate Australian *identity* might develop; that is, a national identity which has something new to offer, something individual to say; an identity intrinsically Australian, based on elements of the culture of the country's indigenous inhabitants.

As contemporary Aboriginal arts have become more prevalent over the last two decades, various "issues" have risen to surround them, some of which are addressed by the artists in this book. What happens when Aboriginal art becomes investment art? Has Aboriginality become fashionable and if so what are the consequences? What is Aboriginality? Many artists argue that they are tired of the "Aboriginal artist" tag. They want their work to be assessed on its quality and not its Aboriginality. They argue that this continual labelling of their art as "Aboriginal" pushes their work back into the margins, when it must, on the contrary, become part of the prevailing Australian psyche. Some people discuss the issues of criticism: are white critics equipped or able to evaluate Aboriginal work? If they are not, who is going to criticise it? Should it be criticised? Many artists talk about the urban/rural division within the Aboriginal community. Is it ethical for urban artists to use traditional imagery?

Is it ethical for white artists to appropriate Aboriginal designs in some form of cross-cultural pollination? Should Aboriginal literature or drama have an intrinsically different form to that of the European? How does the structure of theatre differ? All these questions were raised to varying degrees in the process of people talking about their lives and work.

There are certainly many other viewpoints which could have been included, but unfortunately space was limited. There are several "high profile" artists who do not appear because one of my major goals was to use the space to talk to a diverse range of people. I chose the format of transcribed interviews as the closest thing to "self-representation" possible in a book and returned the edited manuscripts to the artists for approval.

The thirty-one interviews represent different opinions and personal experiences. There are though, common themes which run through them all: the experiences of dispossession and assimilation policies, and the struggle to retain and strengthen cultural links in the face of colonisation. These experiences are expressed, however, with a strong humour, determination, resilience and pride. I hope these voices open up some of the prevailing issues surrounding the development of contemporary Aboriginal arts, and that while doing so they teach other people as much as they have taught me.

WESTERN AUSTRALIA

'Marawali' (detail), Peter Skipper

JACK DAVIS:
Playwright and Poet

Jack's first book of poetry, The First Born, *was published by Angus and Robertson in Sydney in 1970. In 1971 he became the first chairman of the Aboriginal Lands Trust in Western Australia. From 1972 to 1977 he was managing editor of the Aboriginal Publications Foundation; subsequently he established a course for Aboriginal writers at Murdoch University. Jack is also a member of the Aboriginal Arts Board of the Australia Council.*

Kullark, presented in 1979, was his first full-length play and documented the history of Aborginals in Western Australia. The Dreamers *followed in 1983;* No Sugar *and* Honey Spot *(a children's play) in 1985.* No Sugar *was performed in Vancouver in 1986 and received standing ovations.* Barungin — *which looks at the issue of Aboriginal deaths in custody — opened at the Perth Festival in 1988.*

In 1977 Jack Davis received the British Empire Medal for his contribution to Australian literature; in 1985 he became a member of the Order of Australia for his contribution to Australian theatre and also received the Sidney Myer Performing Arts Award for his contribution to the arts. Jack was made an Honorary Doctor of Literature by Murdoch University and was elected Citizen of the Year in Western Australia in 1988. He currently lives and works from his home in Fremantle, Western Australia.

I was born in Perth at King Edward hospital. I was just born there and then I was carted away into the bush. My dad was what you called an itinerant worker in those days, but we eventually finished up at a little place called Yarloop which is about 140 kms south of Perth. He got a permanent job there and lived there until he died. I went to school there until I was fifteen. School was a great time for me, it was a country-town school and had about a hundred-and-fifty children. Yarloop was an isolated community: there weren't so many cars around as there are today and certainly there was no television and very rarely you heard the radio. We all lived in this little town (which was a timber-milling town in the dairy district) and we were quite happy there: we had plenty of bush to play in, a nice school and a freshwater creek that ran through the west of the town. It was a great place for kids to live in.

Our family was intact until the death of our father. I was one of eleven children. I was fifteen when I left home. I roamed around the State for many many years until I settled down in Fremantle; I was in the north-west for seven years working as a stockman, a windmill man, a horse-breaker; when I was in the south I was working on farms, clearing land, cutting down posts, doing anything. The rest of the time I've lived in towns, in civilisation as it were.

My dad used to tell lots of stories and we knew quite a lot about the Aboriginal way of life. We were a closeknit community at Yarloop — the world began and finished at Yarloop for us.

I was a fanciful child, I remember once coming home from school when I was about ten... coming home through the bushes and there was a small tree leaning onto another tree. In my mind the little tree was just leaning against the other one and they were creaking or rubbing against each other. I thought the little tree was a child talking to its mother; so when I got home I said to my mum, "Do you know what happened today? I heard two trees talking." She asked me how that was and — because she was a very astute woman — when I explained she agreed with me. The clover at Yarloop used to grow in wild carpets and when I would lift the clover what I'd see were beetles and insects scurrying away from the light; but I used to think they were fairies and gnomes just turning themselves into beetles so that they could dodge me. I remember other times too — for instance I used to pick mushrooms (everybody ate mushrooms down there in the mushroom season) but if I found that there was a beetle or a grub or something on a mushroom I would put it back on the ground. What I reckoned was that it was the beetle's house or something, I felt I had no right to pick up that mushroom. I wouldn't even kill a snake or anything because I thought that snake might be a mother and then what would happen to its kids?

I was a happy kid, I never felt myself any different from any other child. But, looking back, I think I had a very vivid imagination. It has stood me in good stead as a writer. I like writing about the environment. I think if people took more notice of the environment then the world would be a much better place.

When I got out into the wide world I found that it wasn't what it was supposed to be for me. I ran into lots of discrimination. This didn't worry me, because I was educated and therefore able to counter prejudice, but I saw lots of Aboriginal people who were being discriminated against — not just by the townspeople but by the law itself. I became very angry. As a child I had lived the same life as any white kid but now I found I was classified as being black; I also found that there was a different set of laws which I had to live under. Of course I fought those laws by the only way I

RETROSPECT

When I was small
And oh, so tall
I looked for homes
Of elves and gnomes
Hiding in the clover.

I watched the sun's last gold array
Fade and fold the day away;
I heard the light's last laughing word
From the kookaburra bird;
I heard the wind and winter rains
On the high tin roof and the window panes,
There was little-boy bliss
In a mother's kiss,
Then the day was really over.

Man, don't yearn for the past to return,
The years have all passed over.
I know now there are many things
With hidden stings
Deep down in the clover.

— JACK DAVIS

could — by becoming angry — and so I eventually finished up in jail as a result of my attitude. I had to toe the line but as I grew older I began to fight for justice for the Aboriginal people of my State...

I've been writing poetry since I was about thirteen or fourteen: poetry is a way for me of relieving my feelings. I've been writing plays fairly productively since 1979, but I am in a much happier medium when working as a poet. All Aboriginal writers write about the one thing, which is the way we've had to exist in the last two-hundred years. You cannot divorce Aboriginals today from politics. Of course we write about our own experiences first because they're the ones we know about; really it's always the one theme that we portray. We in the urban areas are stuck: we can't go back, we've practically lost our culture — and yet we can't go forward into the white man's culture.

It wasn't until I turned fifty that I had my first book of poems published. Now I'm one of the recipients of the Federal Government fellowships which gives me $50,000 a year for four years. That's quite good: it means I don't have to worry about applying elsewhere for money — so I've produced quite a large volume of work in the last six months. I think that kind of support should be more readily available for artists. Aboriginal art is one of the most unique forms of art in the world: it *is* the oldest living culture in the world today. I hope in time that the anger disappears or dilutes and that the work will be about building harmonious relations between black and white.

I think Aboriginal art will stand on its own merit anywhere against Aztec art or any art which is practised by indigenous people. There are white artists today who are borrowing Aboriginal techniques and putting them into their paintings. It will happen and you can't do anything about it. On the other side blacks are using pastels and paints and oils which they never used before; and I suppose it really doesn't matter. I mean you can't say to so-and-so, "Well, you can't write about blacks because you're non-Aboriginal." That's just ridiculous. Lots of people today think that Aboriginal literature should be classified as "Aboriginal literature" and written only by blacks. Well, that's rubbish; it's like saying that a black person can only be treated by a black doctor! In my opinion I can write about white situations, European situations — in the same way that white writers can write about black situations...

In terms of criticism, now that's a different issue. I don't think white critics have necessarily shied away from looking at Aboriginal work, what I think is they don't understand it. Many of my actors haven't been trained, they're relatives and friends, and they live out their lives or their friends' lives on stage. My plays deal with an extended family and its day-by-day existence as it struggles to pay the rent, to get the kids to school, to keep things together. The real battlers in my plays are the Aboriginal women — just as it is in real life today. There are no heroes and no heroines. Everyone has an integral part to play and everyone does it extremely well. But none of them are trained actors; they just know about the lifestyles and behavioural patterns and speech patterns of Aboriginal people and they don't have to be told how to act it. Now, if you took my actors and put them into *Twelfth Night,* they'd fail, they'd simply fail. That's why the critics can't make a comment. Critics can't write about something which they're not aware of. Maybe when there are more playwrights, maybe when more Aboriginal plays are being performed, maybe when we have more black and white people performing together... *then* maybe we'll have better criticism. At the moment the critic can go and criticise *Hamlet* or *Othello,* but can't go and criticise *No Sugar* because he doesn't understand why it was formed that way. All he can do is just see that it hurts, that it really hurts...

More people are identifying with Aboriginal art and life. Back in the 1960s most of us adopted parts of the Aboriginal lifestyle — that's where our beachcombers come from, that's where our freethinkers come from. I think a lot of people now realise, "Well, here is a better way of living, we're in a perfect environment for a free and easy lifestyle," and I think this attracts a lot of people back to the Aboriginal philosophy of life. This philosophy swept throughout the world in the 1960s: look at the world of medicine for instance. Aboriginal medicine has been around for at least 40,000 years and is being used in white medicine today.

    People are looking for change now and more and more and more aspects of Aboriginal culture make sense to them. The environment was important to Aboriginal people for thousands and thousands of years and the white man has to realise that if they are going to survive they have to take more care.

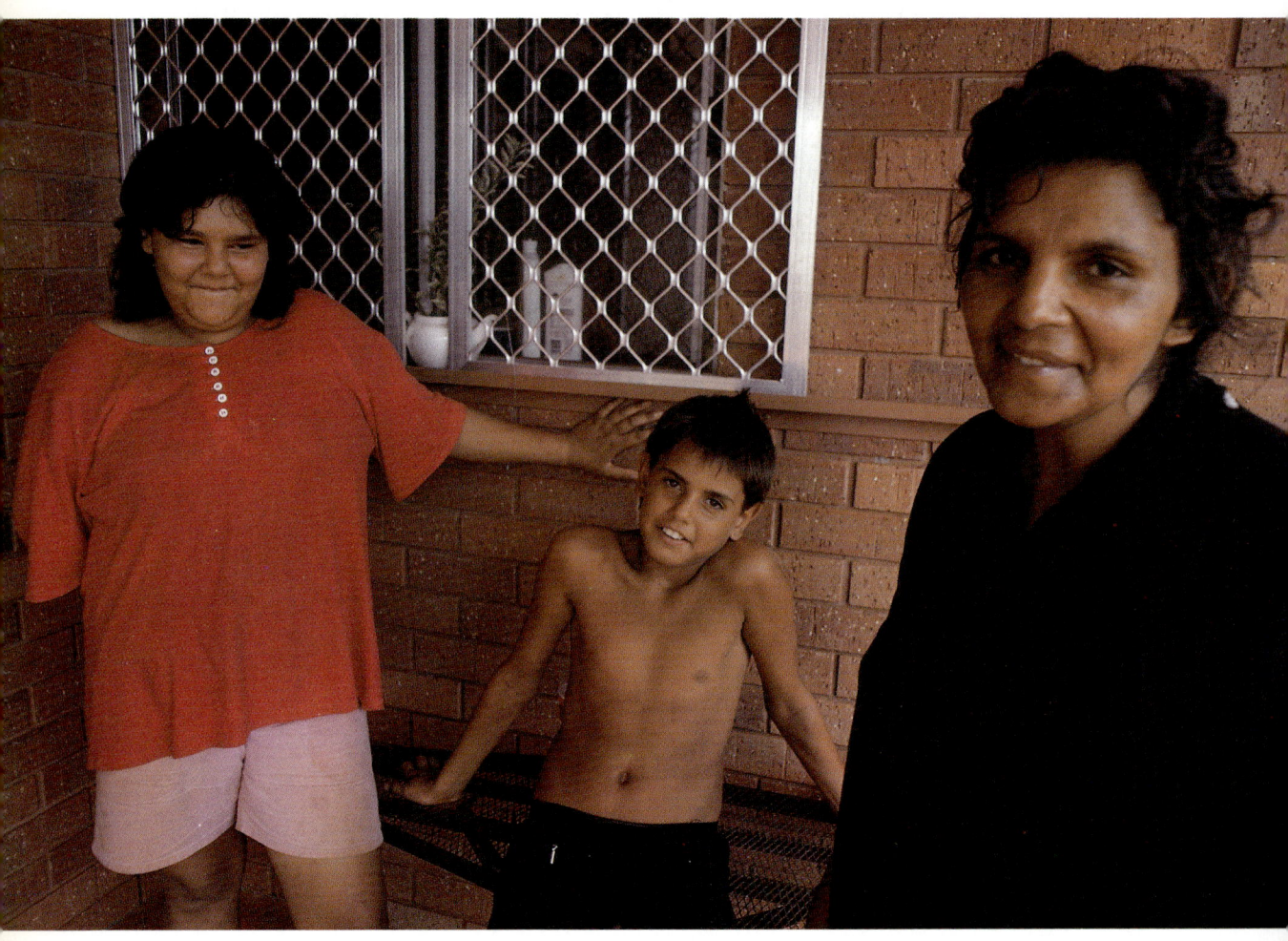

Glenyse Ward with her children, Jodie and Brian at their home in Broome.

GLENYSE WARD: *Writer*

Glenyse Ward was born in 1949 in Perth, Western Australia. She was taken from her parents by Native Welfare at the age of one. Glenyse was put into an orphanage and at the age of three was transferred to the St Francis Xavier Native Mission at Wandering Brook. She was schooled at the mission; and later worked in the fields, dairy and the kitchens until she was sixteen. During all this time she had no contact with her family.

In her book Wandering Girl *Glenyse tells of her experiences during her first year out of the mission.*

Glenyse is currently living in Broome with her husband and two children; she is working on her next book, which is about the life of the children of the mission where she grew up. Glenyse is thinking of calling the book Lux in Tenebris, Light in Darkness, *the Latin logo she wore on the pocket of her school blazer.*

Mum had taken me to a doctor one day: she was sitting in the waiting-room and while she was waiting for me they rang up the Native Welfare people and I was whisked out the back then and there. They told mum to go home where she came from, that she was an unfit mother. Those were the days when no Aboriginal people were allowed in town; they had to be off the street at six o'clock at night and if they weren't then they were jailed. Mum didn't know where I'd gone or what had happened. First I got taken to a place called St Joseph's Orphanage. When I turned three I went out to a place called Wandering Brook. That was the mission that was run by the Germans.

That mission was very strict: boys down one end and girls at the other. We weren't allowed to talk to or to associate ourselves with each other, we had separate playing fields, we sat on opposite sides of the church. Our dresses were all khaki material, right down to the ankle. Where we washed in the laundry, we used old washing boards, tin tubs... of course we had to do all our washing and scrubbing and all that, all our clothes got boiled in the two big coppers the Brothers had made. After school we worked in the laundry or in the dairy, or else we helped the Brothers in the fields.

I was one of twelve kids who never went away for holidays. Whenever Christmas time came there were kids going home to their parents but we just stayed there on our own, with nowhere to go. Still, although we weren't allowed to talk to the boys we had fun.

My strongest memories are when the State schoolteachers came. The nuns were hard, but not hard like those State schoolteachers. I mean they — the nuns — never told us that we were black or that we weren't any good. But the State schoolteachers did, they always made us feel we were no good, they kept telling us we were no good, they were really cruel to us, hitting us with sticks for no reason at all, chucking a duster at us... all that sort of thing. One day this teacher said to write a composition and I wrote a little story and I was really pleased with what I done and I ran up to him and gave it to him and he looked at it and he ripped the pages up and chucked them on the floor and he said "you pick 'em up" and I bent down and he booted me right back to my seat. That memory kept in me all the time but it never discouraged me from writing, in fact it gave me more steam.

I wasn't really aware of my situation, you see. What made me aware of it as the years went by and we got older was that more kids kept coming in, taken from their families. The parents would be told their kids would be better-off educated in a home and going to school and that then they could go back home. That's when I got aware of my own situation — 'cause some of the kids talked about their mums and dads and one of the girls asked me one day "where's your mum" and I looked over to the nun who was standing there over by the corner of the convent and said "that's my mother" and the girl looked over and said "don't be silly she's not your mother" and I said, "'course she is". See, I wasn't aware at all. As the years went by and I got older I started thinking, I must have a mum somewhere along the line...

It was quite incredible when I met up with my mother the first time. It was a bit of a shock for her and I think it took her a long time to realise I was really there you know. I met her in Geraldton walking across the footpath. I happened to be there one day and I looked at her and had that same vision of this lady I knew when I was little. So I just walked up to her and said "hello mum" and she nearly fell over. She got such a shock and she said "who are you" and I said "I'm your daughter Glenyse, I've left the home now." Well, she stood there and she just looked and looked and then she just dropped her bag and burst out crying and gave me a big hug. From there on we kept in touch. Like I said, I had a vision of her in my mind, I still had her picture in my mind through all the years I was growing up.

We'd *all* been taken away, see. I had a brother and he got taken to another home 'cause in those days boys and girls never grew up together. Later on, about twenty years later, when I was nursing in the Home of Peace Hospital my mother came down from Geraldton. She was crying. She said, "Your brother had an accident and he's going to die soon." I'd never seen him — not once in my life. They flew him from Heidelberg Hospital in Melbourne to Shenton Park in Perth. What happened was he was holidaying and jumped into this river to save two boys that were

WANDERING GIRL

I shall never forget one of those lavish parties she threw. All the High Society was there. I remember the preparation I had to put into it — forever cleaning, mopping, shining things up for days. Her daughter came from town to help her mother. I couldn't see any sense in why she came, since I had to do everything.

As well as my cleaning jobs, I had to do all the kitchen duties, like preparing the vegies, washing the pots, pans, cleaning the walls etc, etc... making sure the pantry was spotless, washing and waxing the lino of the kitchen floor — all her daughter did was stir the pots of food on the stove.

I heard her say to her daughter that this party was something to do with elections. I didn't understand what that meant, I just carried on with my work, getting things ready so everything would look nice for her party.

Now on the night, she came to me all done up in a long lime green evening gown. Her daughter was there too, dressed in a silvery white gown. Like her mother she was dainty, with a turned up nose and plenty of rouge and lipstick on. A real *pretty kid*, as we say.

Their necklaces and earrings were of beautiful pale blue colours, but with all that make-up and rouge on, they both looked like clowns. As I'd never seen women dressed up like that it was something new to me — I thought they looked quite comical!

Anyway, she came over to give me strict instructions. When all her guests arrived, I was to take her two grandchildren into the back room — what she used to call the sleepout. I was to look after her grand-kids in that room. I wasn't allowed to show myself to her guests, so she left me and the kids there while she went to greet them.

I settled the kids down. When they fell asleep, I looked out the door — cars were everywhere. I took a look at the kids, they were sound asleep. So I thought I'd better go and help Mrs Bigelow, me feeling sorry for her and thinking she might need a hand with all those people. So kind-hearted me bolded into the V.I.P. room, looking like a real Orphan Annie.

Soon as I opened the door all the chatter and laughter stopped. You could hear a pin drop as all eyes were on me. All of a sudden, some poshed-up voice, with a plum in her mouth, came out of the crowd, 'Tracey dear, is this your little dark servant?'

I just stood there smiling. I thought it was wonderful that at last people were taking notice of me. There were sniggers and jeers from everywhere. I turned to the lady who did all the talking, and said, 'My name is Glenyse'. She was quite startled; she said, 'Oh dear, I didn't think you had a name'.

At the time, I didn't understand what she was going on about. Mrs Bigelow came over to me and said in the sweetest voice, 'It's alright dear, you may go to bed now'.

This was a shock to my system. I thought, 'My luck has changed'. At last she felt sorry for me, which stirred my emotions up, as she ushered me out of the room, and waited till we got out of hearing distance. 'Don't you ever do that to me again!'

I was so taken aback I nearly wet myself. I told her in a very shaky voice that I only wanted to help her. She replied that I had disgraced her in front of all her friends. I went to my room crying with shame and anger.

I lay back on my bed, and began to hate the place and the people in it. I wondered what could be so bad about me?

— GLENYSE WARD

drowning and he landed on his neck, ended up paralysed and crippled. That day when I went up to see him in Perth with my mother she bent over him and said, "Brian this is your sister I was telling you about". He opened his eyes but he couldn't move or anything and when he saw me I said "hello" and I gave him a kiss. I leaned on his chest and that was it: he cried and cried and cried... I only saw him for one week, then he died. That was the only time I had with my brother.

It was very hard really, you know. I realise how my mother felt when they took us away, no wonder she turned out an alcoholic and hit the bottle. Now she's married this white bloke; he took her to church one day, to the Salvation Army. All the times she drank he kept his faith in her and now she's a different woman altogether. She's a very strict religious person now, but I'd rather have her like that than not have her at all. At least I'm seeing her every year and the kids are growing up seeing their nana.

My father got killed while I was in the home. I was playing marbles one day and I was just about to punch this girl 'cause we were having a rip about this one marble that she wouldn't give up when the nun came over and said: "All you girls kneel down where you are." Then she said to me: "Glenyse, we come to say prayers for the dead." Well it never dawned on me you know, it never really hit me that it was *my* father they were praying for. She just said to me: "Say a prayer for your father, he got killed". And then she walked away. That's how she told me about my father, so to this day I don't even know what he looked like.

It would have been good to see my mum and dad and my grandmother, it would have been good to see all of them. Like I said, I suppose they thought I would have been better-off with the Christians — but that's not really what it's like, you know. For my mother there was no other way out but alcohol — when alcohol was introduced to the Aboriginal people well, that was it, wasn't it? — and drinking was the only way for her to cope. It made her worse all that drinking you know, it didn't make her any good really; but I suppose since she's come to the Lord and has found Him she's happy now. Everybody used to drink in those days, all her uncles and aunties and my cousins, they all used to sit around and drink and talk. I suppose that's what helped bring their feelings out. So I don't blame mum for that you know, I don't blame her for anything really.

When I did actually come to leave the mission I went to these white people's home. The white people around the area would ring up the mission to see if there were any girls ready to work, and if you were about thirteen or fourteen and you weren't any good at school anymore the nuns would send you out to work with these people — like slaves. It was all so strange — the way the white woman treated me. I thought, that's how everybody must treat everybody else. I didn't know any other way of life, see. All the time that I was with that woman I felt like a zombie, like I was walking around like a ghost. Everything was so secure when I was living at the mission but now there was nobody there, I was just on my own. It was just like being put in a cage, like you're a bird and then all of a sudden you're set free and you don't know where to fly to or what's going on. So eventually I left these white people, I ran away.

In my book *Wandering Girl* there are bits about the mission but really it's about my life when I left it. No-one taught me how to write. I just put things down on paper. Ever since I was a little girl I'd write down what I thought and kept the bits of paper under my pillow or whatever. As the years went by I kept doing that and even when I worked for that white woman I was sort of putting things down.

This book that I'm writing now is about Wandering Brook, the mission itself. The reason I want to write about it is because there's a lot of white people who've heard you went to homes but they don't know about how you grew up with the nuns. I think it's important that they *do* know. I can't speak for other people but I can speak for myself — and I'm not really angry but I'll never forget the past. Being angry now won't achieve anything.

Perhaps I'm going to achieve something through my writing. Perhaps I can bring my feelings out that way, and perhaps people can understand. I mean I'm not a really hard sort of person and I do see the funny side of things — though it wasn't funny at the time. But I'm thinking about my background, how other people went through worse than what I did. I think the only way I'm going to get through to other people is through literature, through books. I think I'll get the message across that way better than being hard about it. I don't think a lot of people realise that there's a whole lot of history involving real sadness — a lot of broken families, a lot of families split up.

Since *Wandering Girl* a lot of people have come to me and said: "I've read your book, could you help me with this and could you help me with that, help me write a book?" And I say, "Yes, well, come along and I'll give you all the help I can." I hope a lot of kids follow behind me and that the older ones who are interested in writing put their history down. Once the old people go, everything's gone. If we bring up our kids the right way and set them in the right frame of mind and let them know that we're all the same — that there's no-one different in this world, that we're all the same whether black or white — then if we can get that through their heads and everyone else's that we should all live as one race . . . well, that would be a good thing now, wouldn't it?

JIMMY CHI:
Musician and Songwriter

Jimmy Chi is the author of the recent musical Bran Nue Dae *which opened to standing ovations at the Perth Festival in early 1990 and quickly brought him into the public arena.* Bran Nue Dae *draws strongly on songs written and produced by the band "Kuckles", of which Jimmy is a member.* Bran Nue Dae *is considered to be the first mainstream Aboriginal musical.*

"Kuckles" has recorded some of their work at the Centre for Aboriginal Studies in Music in Adelaide, South Australia, and the band was selected to travel and play in Cologne, Germany. Jimmy (with Mick Manolis) has produced a book on Aboriginal music which was published by Hodger in 1983. He was involved in the founding of the Broome Musicians Aboriginal Corporation, which, amongst other things, provides support for young musicians and places a strong emphasis on community entertainment. Jimmy is currently living and working in Broome, Western Australia.

I was born in Broome in 1948 of a Japanese-Chinese father and of an Aboriginal-Scottish mother and went to school at St Mary's in Broome – a Catholic school run by Irish nuns. School was wonderful but I was subjected to racism – often from black, predominantly tribal, schoolmates. Even though I was related to them they never realised it: they used to call me *munyi munyi* – meaning eye, slanty-eyed if you want. I've had racism from whites, from blacks, from everybody just about...

A lot of people in traditional society don't see me as Aboriginal, certainly in the Eastern states they don't. Even in Broome there's social classes which go first white, then coloured, then blackfella and bush blackfella, then the absolute nigger, and last the ignorant stonejack. The whole thing about prejudice like that is that it runs through all levels of society and that Aboriginal people are as guilty of it as anybody else. In fact all people are – Aboriginals, whites, whoever. Ultimately I regard myself as a human being who has the right to do whatever I want to do provided it doesn't hurt anybody. People have to be concerned about all the issues that affect us in our lives and they have to try to be part of the solution rather than part of the problem.

In some respects I can't come to terms with my own Aboriginality. I'd like to research my language, my culture on the Aboriginal side – but at the same time I'd like to research those other ethnic groups that I belong to as well. I think to become a complete human being you've got to look at the history of all your composites. I feel I can make a contribution to Australia, as an Aboriginal. I can't say I'm Asian, I can't say I'm Chinese, I can't say I'm Scottish. I *can* say I'm Aboriginal; but will the Aboriginal people themselves look on me as Aboriginal?

It doesn't mean that just because I can identify with being an Aboriginal, it is necessarily any easier for me. You're still confronted with the same problems, so really first you have to accept yourself as a human being and believe you have a worthwhile contribution to make. This will never happen unless Australians are able to realise they have a lot to learn from the ethnic groups here. What they forget is that they have this convict heritage, they forget all that their forefathers went through. They also forget that they in turn went and pillaged and raped somebody else's land. So they need to really look at history to find out their own place in the world and in the scheme of things.

I helped on a thesis with Ernest Hunter — a psychiatrist researching Aboriginal suicide. Suicide is a world trend with indigenous peoples, wherever there's a white majority. The main reason for it has a lot to do with a complete shattering of indigenous peoples' egos by prejudice: eventually they just crack under it. Add to this bad nutrition and the squalid conditions they live under, which just goes on from one generation to the next. I'm talking about indigenous peoples' sense of worth, their identity, I suppose.

My direction changed when I developed schizophrenia after a car accident while I was at Quinos University studying engineering. After the accident I couldn't continue with university; I just broke down a number of times, then finally realised it was pointless to even attempt to continue because I was so sick. Music was my therapy — a comfort, a spiritual source I found that made me write about all the pain that was in me about a lot of issues, and helped me relate to the world again. When I was at university I realised how much bullshit there was in the history that was taught in schools. As an angry young man I became concerned about it, I wanted to go out shooting people; but my anger at last got tempered by my illness. This is good: with hate you only kill *yourself* — and what I've learnt is you've got to love.

For the past twenty years I've been struggling with schizophrenia, with keeping my sanity by writing music and by being involved in Aboriginal and community affairs. I got severely burnt when I was about three; I almost died then... So I've been coping with hospitals and with institutionalisation ever since; all my life, just about. I've thought about

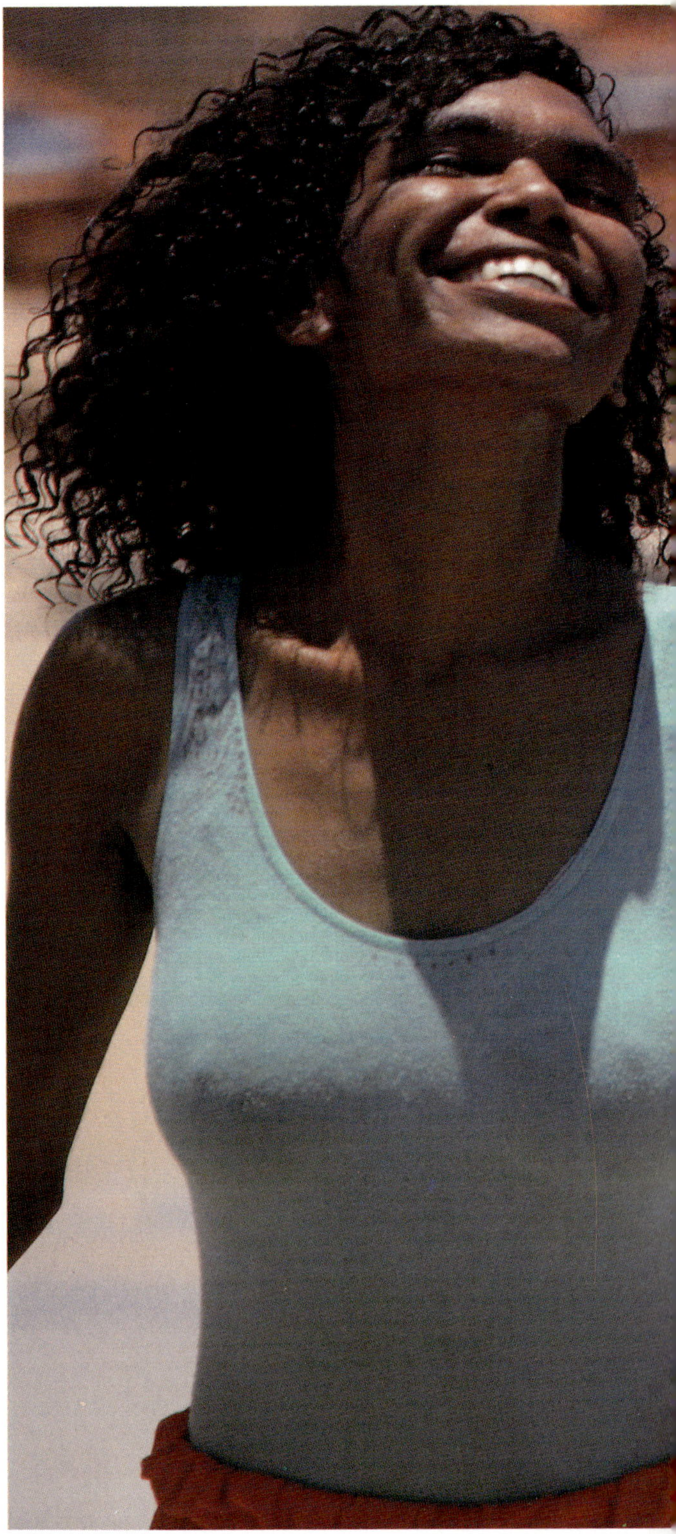

**Above: Jimmy Chi in Broome.
Right: Dancer Jose Lawford and
Bran Nue Dae cast rehearsing
on Cable Beach Broome.**

NOTHING I WOULD RATHER BE

Nothing I would rather be
than to be an Aborigine
and watch you take my precious land away
For nothing gives me greater joy than to
watch you fill each girl and boy
with superficial existential shit,

(Chorus:)
Now you may think I'm cheeky
but I'd be satisfied
to rebuild your convict ships
and sail you on the tide.

I love the way you give me God
and of course the mining board
for this of course I thank the Lord
each day.
I'm glad you say that land rights wrong
then you should go where you belong
and leave me to just keep on keeping on.

— **JIMMY CHI AND
KUCKLES BAND**
(From *Bran Nue Dae*)

suicide a number of times. My struggle with schizophrenia has been very hard: at the Indian Ocean Festival, for example, I had to go and sleep before coming on to perform, just because of the effects of the drugs. I've been hospitalised a few times. Once I nearly died because they gave me the wrong medication and this sent me deeper into the illness, into a world that's quite frightening. I've had shock treatment of course.

I've also been taken out on a plane in a straightjacket . . . but I don't regret having had that experience because I think it's given me a kind of sensitivity, it's helped me to write what I do write about and it makes me more loving and more tempered in terms of caring for other people and trying to live as well as I can. All the experiences I have had have made me what I am: more concerned about the world, trying to alleviate the suffering and all the problems that I see. I may not do that — sometimes I may not be the best person, but I'm trying.

Now I work with "Kuckles", our band with Stevie Pigram and Mick Manolis whom I met in 1975 after the Darwin cyclone. The music we've been writing over the last few years is a focus for a lot of peoples' sense of pride and concern. It puts them in contact with one another, it gives them hope I suppose — as well as an opportunity to come together and to resolve a lot of problems in the community at large. One song we wrote featured during the Nukanbah situation: we got in the back of a truck and sang this song and that went all over the world in 1980. It was written about 1975/6, it means a lot to Aboriginal people in terms of what it says. The members of "Kuckles" and myself have been working especially at a community level. We're caught up with a lot of community issues; our material comes from how we see the world — whether it's AIDS, or Vietnam, or whatever.

The play which is now happening is a vehicle for the songs written by the members of "Kuckles". Hopefully people will listen to songs like 'Nothing I would rather be than to be an Aborigine'. There's songs like 'Listen to the News' which is a comment on Aboriginal deaths in custody and on the imprisonment of blacks by police. 'Listen to the News' is also a song about the Second Coming — not in the Christian sense but in the sense that there's this New Messiah that's going to come. He's going to come — this is what I believe — in about the year 2000, the dawning of the Golden Age.

People laughed when I left university and said I was going to be a musician. Writing *Bran Nue Dae* with Mick changed a lot of peoples' ideas about their capabilities. It's the first-ever Aboriginal musical produced by Aboriginal people. It uses a lot of religious and spiritual symbols from traditional to Eastern to Judaeo-Christian sources to make people see basically that they are *spiritual* beings, that the physical world is not the reality but an illusion, that the world has to get back to God and spiritual values before it can advance. I'm attempting to show Aboriginal spirituality by showing the true character of Aboriginal people, by showing how their life can be simple — whether it's the life of the old drunks or of my old grannies. I'm attempting to show that you just have to accept yourself. Acceptance is part of truth, this is what happens in the finale of *Bran Nue Dae.* You don't have to be anything, there's another day, a brand new day, so don't worry about today, just live one day at a time; if something's bad then forget about it — there'll be another day, forget about the past. Look to the future and stay right in the now, live in the now and don't criticise yourself, don't be too hard on yourself, realise your own humanity. That's what I'm trying to paint in this thing, what I've learnt of Aboriginal spirituality anyway.

I think things will change as history is being rewritten. I think that writing and theatre and music have a lot to do with changing peoples' attitudes. We need a lot more people — not just Aboriginal people but also other people who are willing — to work not only for Australia but for the world so as to change opinion. There needs to be white writers writing about it too, and white artists and white activists.

It's interesting that a lot of the Aboriginal people involved in this work have not had any formal training, and yet they are the leaders in their respective fields of work. I haven't had any formal training in music, Jack Davis hasn't had any formal training in theatre, Mudrooroo Narogin has had no formal training in writing and neither has Archie Weller; so it's got nothing to do with education — it's just a concern, I think. They're just maintaining the pressure to try and educate the white people and show that Aboriginal people *do* have a place in this society, a *rightful* place and an *honoured* place in Australian history. I don't think they're working for it for any other reason. People, whether they're white or black, can do whatever they want to do as long as they believe in themselves. That's all it is, it's that belief, that's what got me here, that's what has kept me alive.

Paddy Roe with his wife at their home in Broome.

PADDY ROE: *Storyteller*

Paddy Roe was born at Roebuck Plain Station around 1912. He came to Broome during World War Two. He is one of the traditional custodians of the land around Broome and is currently trying to establish a "Heritage Trail" in order to protect threatened sacred sights.

Paddy tells many stories of his life and his feelings about the changes he sees around him. Some of these stories have been recorded and transcribed by Stephen Muecke to produce Paddy's books, Reading the Country *and* Gularubulu. *Paddy believes it is very important to pass on such stories to both black and white people in the hope that it will bring the two cultures closer together and contribute to a consciousness of the importance of our environment.*

He is a highly respected figure and used to hold small gatherings at his home in Broome, where he performed traditional dance and related stories to the local community.

My name's Paddy Roe, I was born in Roebuck Plain station, just out of Broome, 1912. I live in the bush for long time, I live in the bush, yes. In the bush, very good life, very good life, very happy there. I don't stay in the station, but when we was out in the bush we go hunting everyday, when I come back I got job on the station, they gave me job on the station. I was only a little boy then but I grow up then on the station, I grow up, then I was a man, so I run the station too while my boss go back to America, he's from America this bloke I used to work with, you know my boss . . .

Wartime I come in, they bring me in from the station. The army was here, when this place was bombed. Japanese. That's the time everyone run away from Broome.

I went working in the slaughteryard then. Slaughter man, slaughtering bullock meat for the army. Only about two people was left: one bloke working in the hotel and me working in the butcher. I was never frightened for whatsaname — you know, if we get killed or not . . . bomb . . . machine-gun . . . anything like that. They dropped a bomb very close to us one time . . . one night they dropped about six or seven bombs but nothing went off. We was very lucky.

Broome has changed a lot today, it's not the same, getting bigger and bigger all the the time. When I was small boy — pearlers were here. Broome was alright: lots of Chinese, Japanese, all sorts of people. Filipinos and Malaysians, Kopangs, all, lot of people all mix. We used to work together, no worries at all. We was happy those days.

I look after this land round Broome now, I was well-trained for that, bottom and top. This land is everything from Bogadagada – English say Dreamtime. I look after the Dreamtime stories today. That was my education when I was a young fella. I went through my law and I know these things, I come from the true people in this country in Roebuck Plain. There was about sixty or seventy old people here. These old people used to say, "You must look after this one they tell me, you sit down now under the tree, you must look after this one." "Oh yes," I say, "What is it?" "Oh that's where you get your fish from when the tide's out. You must look after it." They tell me everything, right through. "This stone, you must look after it," they say, "because this one's from Bogadagada, that one's a statue." And then they sing to me, they sing to me, they say you must look after them.

I said to my lady, I think I better ask these old fellas, I said, I think they might be mad these old fellas. So I asked. "I'm going to ask you people," I said. "Yes you can ask," one old man tell me. I was very close to him, that one old fella. "All right," I said, "what make you people think this country going to be mine, that I goin' to look after it? You blokes tell me about this country all the way when we was comin up." "Can't you see," they tell me. "No I can't see," I tell them. "Alright, we tell you. You see that old man?" they tell me. "And you see us, we won't have any more kids, we too old, we just going to die like this, so this country is yours, we give you it now."

I put my head down you know, I believed and I didn't believe you know. That's why that country was given to me by the old people, that's true too. These old people when they die, they left the country with me. Now some people always ask, "Did they leave it in writing?" "Don't ask silly question," I say, "Who going to read that paper? *I* can't read, I never been to school, them old people never been to school either, so what's the good? It's all in here, in here, in brain, in here," I tell them, "Don't ask silly question."

It is the country of the Rainbow Serpent, Yunguru. I belong to one of them, that's where I come from, that's my helper. If I want to stop the rain, I stop the rain; if I want to get the rain, I get the rain. I can tell you every little inch of this land, the water holes and stones and everything from Bogadagada.

Nobody got these things so today I'm passing these things onto my young generation. I got twenty-nine grandchildren, fifty-six and a half great-grandchildren, one's not out yet. Lot of people never pass things over to people before, you know, that's why there's always argument. Today I tell them, I'm passing these things over to my young generation and I'm passing these things over to Europeans too, to come more close together.

Children, they're the ones I'm looking at, not me, they must grow together and look after the country, this country now. I never talk all over the country, but I talk for the country what the old people left with me, because it's for all of us to walk in and lay down and walk out, every one of us, black and white...

Everything I know in here children learn if we take 'em round proper way. It was same, someone took us around. In those days they had more time to teach us. We had nothing to do in the night-time. Today is a bit hard for the children. They got to go to basketball, they got to go to football, they got to go to this, they got to go to something else. We look around, where are they, oh they gone, oh well what am I doin here, I better go to sleep then. Drink a problem too, my grandchildren, they have to be sober and listen, quiet, I got to have very quiet place to teach the children. They can ask question, that's alright, but sometimes they ask question bad way, because they're drunk. Drunken men bring bad example to the children. I don't know what the best way but you can't stop those sort of things, that's very stupid. But, that's the trouble we having today, I don't think it's going to get any better, it's gonna get worse, but I won't see that (laughs) I'll be down in the ground then. That's why we try to teach these people culture, culture is very good helper, we must respect that man. I know in our ways, he's old man, you must look after him. I don't know what it's like on the European side, that's the problem, 'Oh he's just an old man, cut his throat', there's all this you see.

I got this heritage trail you know, to teach people, that's the thing. Heritage trail is Bogadagada. This is for people to learn about the country and how to live. This is a time, we must tell people, don't touch that tree, don't touch that stone, don't touch that hill. You can have that one but not that one because that's Bogadagada, from Bogadagada, it's the Dreamtime.

My books are to teach people. Everything that I'm talking about now, they must know. The country, how to live, where to find water, what's in the bush. How to get food. Wild fruit and fish in the sea, outside and inside, all those sort of things are in my books, all in books now, in my two books anyway.

ARCHIE WELLER:
Playwright and Poet

Archie Weller was born in 1957 at King Edward Memorial hospital in Subiaco, Western Australia. He grew up in Cranbrook — a small country town outside Perth.

He finished secondary education and spent a year at the Western Australian Institute of Technology (WAIT). Then he began to write. His first book was Day of the Dog. *Since then he has written* Going Home *and co-edited (with Colleen Francis-Glass)* Us Fellas *— an anthology of Aboriginal writings.*

Archie has also written a considerable amount of poetry. Much of his work is concerned with his experiences as an urban Aboriginal and with the kind of identity struggles he has dealt with. He currently lives in Sydney and is working on a new science-fiction novel.

I grew up on a farm two-hundred miles out of Perth in a place called Cranbrook. My dad's grandmother's people are Aboriginal so I'm not very dark. I actually didn't know that I was Aboriginal until I was eighteen — well, I *did* know but I didn't have any basic feeling about it. My father never told me anything about my being Aboriginal; my mother never told me anything about being Aboriginal either until I was about eighteen. I sort of guessed it, you know; it was the old Aboriginal fellas in the parks and the pubs who were telling me... I don't think my father's very proud of it; I don't think he even really knows himself. It goes back a long way and obviously he must know but he's put it behind him.

It's actually quite interesting that since the Bicentenary so many people have been coming out and saying, "Oh it's great, I discovered I've got an Aboriginal great-great-grandfather or great-great-grandmother." Accepting I was Aboriginal was a really big change for me because the rest of the family doesn't really accept it, my sisters and brother don't accept it. I respect their individuality but I know where I'm going, I'm really proud. I can remember when my grandmother died, she was about ninety-six and I was three and I woke up screaming in my bed and it's my belief that she passed on her spirit to me, you see. The thing is, I get lots of trouble from Aboriginal people as well. But I just tell 'em, I don't care what you call me, I'm Archie Weller and I am Scottish, Irish, Jewish and Spanish, Aboriginal, English, German, but the blood that shines through mostly is

Aboriginal. I always tell people it doesn't matter, the colour of your skin. If you've got the heart and spirit of an Aboriginal, it can never die.

I started writing when I was about twelve years old, after being on the farm. When I write my stories I'm just writing them for myself basically. I go mad if I don't write my books — I gotta do something, people are coming into my head and I gotta get 'em out you know. I used my imagination and made up little characters in my head, and that carried on and I started writing stories. It was beautiful — you're sitting there in a whole little world... you can go anywhere you want to go, be whatever you want to be. I didn't have many friends on the farm and I was really, really shy and I feel myself more at home with the characters I invent. In my stories I write about people like me — people with red hair and green eyes or blonde hair and blue eyes, but they're still Aboriginal. I hope people never ever forget that Aboriginal people are all different colours, all different. You see on TV, you see in the movies, you see David Gulpilil — a great dancer, a good person — but you never ever see the *urban* mob and that's what I'm writing about. I'm interested in *relationships,* not just *human* relationships — but also relationships to do with *land.* Love for land, that's a recurring theme all the way through. Another theme is being a loner because there's quite a few lonely people out there — you can go to parties anywhere in the world and you finish up meeting the old fellas in the pub with their middy and they sit on that middy all day and they're lonely people.

I was first published by Uncle Jack in *Aboriginal Islander Identity.* He was one of the people who got me out of where I was going which was right down the gutter. I was drinking about two flagons of wine a day, just getting real bad. When I was about seventeen or eighteen, I went to try and sell him one of my stories and he said, "I don't want to even look at your stories, you got talent and you should keep that talent, it was given to you as a gift," he said, "I'm going to give you ten dollars out of my pocket. You go and buy a feed of chicken, get something to eat." When you drink wine, you don't eat nothing you know, you just drink all day. And so I did — I went and got me mate and we bought a chicken and I never since that day have drunk port again.

I entered a competition and was runner-up and the story was published by Allen and Unwin and I just went from there. I wrote *Day of the Dog* in six weeks; that book was published and sold a fair amount — it was number four on the bestseller list for six weeks and it's been published now in Holland and America and they're going to make a film out of it. I've been

THE STORM

Eli Johnson climbed up the elevator on to the Wheatbin roof. Actually, this was the coarse grain silo, where barley or lupins were stored. He felt so near to the glorious, dark shapes in the sky, and he wasn't lonely anymore. The wind whipped through the air and tore at his clothes and hair. It beat a song of war upon the loose sheets of iron on the main silo, and the cloud-men, in their purple ochre, danced a frenzied dance of death. Eli dropped down into the mountain of pale, smooth, lupin seeds, and spreading out a tarp, lay on top of them, just below the hole in the roof where the Grain Elevator spewed out the seed. He rolled himself a number and prepared himself to enjoy the storm, in his own way. He dragged the sweetness back inside his body and relaxed. He smiled. He saw a rooster, with a lot of tail feathers, being chased by a long-necked dragon, spitting mist. A purple-black snake poked its head through the hole in the roof and flickered at him. A fat juicy drop of rain like one of those fabled purple grapes that were always out of the fox's reach, splattered on his cheek.

— ARCHIE WELLER

working on a film pretty heavily. I'm also writing a science-fiction book. It's got three very strong Aboriginal characters in it (the rest are white fellas) and it's using very powerful Aboriginal legends — it's more like fantasy really. It's set 15,000 years after the nuclear bomb holocaust, so it's not science fiction — it's still on earth — but it's bringing in Aboriginal legends and the Aboriginal respect for the land; it's bringing in Aboriginal respect for the old people, Aboriginal respect for basic humanity.

The people I'd like to educate are the really deadset rednecks who sit in the pubs talking about Abos and niggers and boongs and all that sort of stuff and not in a blue fit would they go and see Uncle Jack's play — the people who go and see Uncle Jack's play are people who've already been converted. That's the sad thing. It's true that bad things have happened in this country, but it's no good saying your great-grandfather killed my great-grandfather and we're never going to talk, you know — what you got to do is sit down and acknowledge that, and say we come from this particular history here and you come from this history here... in the old days it was Aboriginal history versus white history but it's all just history. It's what builds the country and the past; it builds *people* and whole *societies* you know. We have to look forward now to the *future*.

You have to be careful, because what can happen is that the past can become commercialised, eh? Like, as an example, black deaths in custody: all of a sudden everybody's writing plays about black deaths in custody. The people who *should* write them are people like Uncle Jack and people like me. In my play *Sunset and Shadows* I've got a scene about black deaths in custody, and I don't sort of say, "Oh, the policeman killed him", but at the same time it's a very very personal play, because at the time I wrote it (ten years ago) my girlfriend was killed in prison.

But if the whole issue becomes too commercialised people are just going to say, "Oh it's just another black death in custody," and it all goes right over their heads whereas for me, it will never *ever* go over *my* head because it's a dead set personal thing that happened to me, see. And that goes for everything: it goes for losing your land, it goes for watching your mother drink herself to death, your father drink himself to death, watching your kids get taken away... It didn't happen to me, but it happened to quite a few people I know — walking down the street very happy, cops stop, you're in the back of the van, they give you a good hiding.

It really should make me very very bitter, but I don't get bitter. I just say to myself, well you've had your bit of a time, but I'm going to put you in the story you see, and the pen's more powerful than the sword...

That's the story that Uncle Jack taught me.

SALLY MORGAN: Writer and Artist

Sally Morgan was born in 1950 in Western Australia. She was told by her mother and grandmother that she was Indian. Their own experiences had so instilled in them the difficulties and social implications of being "Aboriginal" that they attempted to protect their children from such negative experiences by totally denying their Aboriginal heritage.

Sally Morgan's first and very successful book, My Place, *tells of her early experiences. Sally's subsequent novel* Wanamurraganya, *recounts the life of her grandfather Jack McPhee.*

As well as for her writing, Sally is well-known for her art work and bold, stylised prints. She currently lives and works from her home in Fremantle.

I grew up in Perth, WA. One of the strongest recollections of my childhood is the bush — playing in the bush, being in the bush, being part of a natural environment. Another recollection is my father being an alcoholic, my grandmother teaching us about plants and trees and things like that, and my mum's sense of humour...

When we were kids people used to ask us what country we came from — and it was only that people *kept* asking us that we realised there was something different about us. It wasn't until I was a teenager that I actually realised that my grandmother was black! Prior to that I hadn't actually noticed, that made me start questioning things then.

I think the reason for my grandmother's denial of our Aboriginality was her life experiences. She'd had a lot of hurt and rejection, her life had been controlled by welfare and government authorities and she had a great fear that we'd be taken away and she wouldn't have us in her life.

Initially, anger about these kinds of things motivated me for *My Place:* I wanted a record for my children so they wouldn't grow up ignorant. From talking to white Australians, I found that no-one knew what the history was — people were incredibly ignorant about Aboriginal people and I wanted to inform them in a personal way, so that they could understand.

There's two sides to the research of *My Place*. Firstly, because I was in the book myself, I had to research my own memory and that took many years, remembering parts of my childhood. (I had to really discipline myself because during that time I had a couple of kids and my grandmother died

MY PLACE

Towards the end of the school year, I arrived home early one day to find Nan sitting at the kitchen table, crying. I froze in the doorway, I'd never seen her cry before.

'Nan... what's wrong?'

'Nothin'!'

'Then what are you crying for?'

She lifted up her arm and thumped her clenched fist hard on the kitchen table. 'You bloody kids don't want me, you want a bloody white grandmother. I'm black. Do you hear, black, black, black!' With that, Nan pushed back her chair and hurried out to her room. I continued to stand in the doorway, I could feel the strap of my heavy schoolbag cutting into my shoulder, but I was too stunned to remove it.

For the first time in my fifteen years, I was conscious of Nan's colouring. She was right, she wasn't white. Well, I thought logically, if she wasn't white, then neither were we. What did that make us, what did that make me? I had never thought of myself as being black before.

That night, as Jill and I were lying quietly on our beds, looking at a poster of John, Paul, George and Ringo, I said, 'Jill... did you know Nan was black?'

'Course I did.'

'I didn't. I just found out.'

'I know you didn't. You're really dumb, sometimes. God, you reckon I'm gullible, some things you just don't see.'

'Oh...'

'You know we're not Indian, don't you?' Jill mumbled.

'Mum said we're Indian.'

'Look at Nan, does she look Indian?'

'I've never really thought about how she looks. Maybe she comes from some Indian tribe we don't know about.'

'Ha! That'll be the day! You know what we are, don't you?'

'No, what?'

'Boongs, we're Boongs!' I could see Jill was unhappy with the idea.

It took a few minutes before I summoned up enough courage to say, 'What's a Boong?'

'A Boong. You know. Aboriginal. God, of all things, we're Aboriginal.'

'Oh.' I suddenly understood. There was a great deal of social stigma attached to being Aboriginal at our school.

'I can't believe you've never heard the word Boong', she muttered in disgust. 'Haven't you ever listened to the kids at school? If they want to run you down, they say, "Aah, ya just a Boong". Honestly, Sally, you live the whole of your life in a daze!'

Jill was right. I did live in a world of my own. She was much more attune to our social environment. It was important for her to be accepted at school, because she enjoyed being there. All I wanted to do was stay home.

'You know, Jill', I said after a while, 'if we are Boongs, and I don't know if we are or not, but if we are, there's nothing we can do about it, so we might as well just accept it.'

'Accept it? Can you tell me one good thing about being an Abo?'

'Well, I don't know much about them', I answered. 'They like animals, don't they? We like animals.'

'A lot of people like animals, Sally. Haven't you heard of the RSPCA?'

'Of course I have! But don't Abos feel close to the earth and all that stuff?'

'God, I don't know. All I know is none of my friends like them. You know, I've been trying to convince Lee for two years that we're Indian.' Lee was Jill's best friend and her opinions were very important. Lee loved Nan, so I didn't see that it mattered.

'You know Susan?' Jill said, interrupting my thoughts. 'Her mother said she doesn't want her mixing with you because you're a bad influence. She reckons all Abos are a bad influence.'

'Aaah, I don't care about Susan, never liked her much anyway.'

'You still don't understand, do you?' Jill groaned in disbelief. 'It's a terrible thing to be Aboriginal. Nobody wants to know you, not just Susan. You can be Indian, Dutch, Italian, anything, but not Aboriginal! I suppose it's all right for someone like you, you don't care what people think. You don't need anyone, but I do!' Jill pulled her rugs over her head and pretended she'd gone to sleep. I think she was crying, but I had too much new information to think about to try and comfort her. Besides, what could I say?

Nan's outburst over her colouring and Jill's assertion that we were Aboriginal heralded a new phase in my relationship with my mother. I began to pester her incessantly about our background. Mum was a hard nut to crack and consistently denied Jill's assertion. She even told me that Nan had come out on a boat from India in the early days. In fact, she was so convincing I began to wonder if Jill was right after all.

When I wasn't pestering Mum, I was busy pestering Nan. To my surprise, I discovered that Nan had a real short fuse when it came to talking about the past. Whenever I attempted to question her, she either lost her temper and began to accuse me of all sorts of things, or she locked herself in her room and wouldn't emerge until it was time for Mum to come home from work. It was a conspiracy.

One night, Mum came into my room and sat on the end of my bed. She had her This Is Serious look on her face. With an unusual amount of firmness in her voice, she said quietly, 'Sally, I want to talk to you'.

I lowered my *Archie* comic. 'What is it?'

'I think you know, don't act dumb with me. You're not to bother Nan any more. She's not as young as she used to be and your questions are making her sick. She never knows when you're going to try and trick her. There's no point in digging up the past, some things are better left buried. Do you understand what I'm saying? You're to leave her alone.'

— **SALLY MORGAN**

and her brother died and there were a lot of family things going on. For some of the time my husband was unemployed and we were broke — we were so broke at one stage that I had to type on both sides of the paper because I couldn't afford to go and buy typing paper. Whenever I felt like giving up, something made me go back to it — I don't know what it was — and then I'd get inspired again.)

The other side of the research was doing archival research — I had to try and access files on my grandmother and on Jack, and they were incredibly hard to get hold of. In WA, and from my understanding in *most* states in Australia, the Welfare Department maintained personal files on all Aboriginal people who had some European ancestry in them, who were fathered somewhere along the line by a white man. The files are very detailed — people's movements, work habits, attitudes, their relationships, who they talked to, what they said... in some instances there's even comments on people's sexual morality. All those kinds of things. The longest one I've got so far is Jack's which is three-hundred pages long.

I think I could do without the publicity the book has attracted. I find it very hard because basically I'm a private person; there's a part of me that's very shy. Even though people don't think that's true, it is, so I find it very hard to speak in public and to be a public person. Sometimes I just want to escape. At the same time, I think the book needed to be written and I think lots more books like it need to be written.

What I'd like to do next is write a novel to be adapted for film. We've had a lot of film offers for *My Place* but I'm not really interested in any of them because the story's still too close to my family, and I don't think we could cope with seeing ourselves on the screen. At the same time, I think there's a real need for work opportunities for Aboriginal actors and actresses in the film industry and within theatre, because we need to get a positive public image. So, I thought if I could write a novel about Aboriginal issues, one that's not directly about my family but one that's drawn from my experiences and the experiences of other people then that would be a great opportunity to make it into a film — *that's* what I'd like to do over the next five years.

I think books are important for people who can read, but the difficulty with my people is a lot of us can't read, and we can't write, and that's why other mediums are important — like cassette tapes, and we're desperately short of things like that. I'd like to see other Aboriginal people — men and women — take up their pens or their cassette recorders and do it themselves — not to think that they can't do it, not to think that their story's not worthwhile, but to put down what their *own* history and life experiences are so that their kids can have that as part of their heritage.

PETER SKIPPER: *Artist*

Peter Skipper was born in about 1929 at Payinjarra in Juwaliny country in the Great Sandy Desert. In his early twenties he and Jimmy Pike walked out of the desert and began working on sheep and cattle stations in the South Kimberley. In the 1960s Peter moved into Fitzroy Crossing, where he and his wife Jukana joined linguists in translating the Bible and compiling a Walmajarri to English dictionary.

Peter started painting in the early 1980s using boards and acrylic paints. The designs that he uses in his work describe traditional stories as well as maps, waterholes and sandhills and journeys.

Peter's work Jila Japingka II *(1987) was included in the 1988 "Dreamings" exhibition for the Asia Society of New York organised in conjunction with the museum of South Australia. He has been involved in several exhibitions including a one-man show at the Craft Centre Gallery, Brisbane; the exhibition "Balance 1990" at the Queensland Art Gallery; "Contemporary Aboriginal Art" at Harvard; and a show at the Chesser Gallery in Adelaide. Peter currently lives and works in Fitzroy Crossing.*

I draw all the things from my home. I draw all the living water and sandhills, the soak water and *Japingka* (waterhole). I draw all the Billabong water and the caves in the hill, and all the trees – everything, right through, I draw in my picture. When I lay near a sandhill I draw my picture in the sand.

I became a man in the desert. My mother and father showed me everything: they showed lizard, showed me snake and little goanna, every animal there in the desert. My mother and father taught me everything. We didn't have tents, so when the big rain comes two fellas they dig a hole they make fork sticks stand up and cover them with spinifex, then they cover it with mud, make a dry place inside. When the rain comes it can't go through: we call this *mangkaja;* maybe white man calls it a house. We live inside it.

Today I live in a house. We've got one room that I can go in when the rain comes: the water can't come through cement. It can rain and rain and water can't come through. When the rains finish we walk around. After the Wet the season is good for hunting: lots of cats, little lizards, goanna.

When I came in from the desert everyone had told me you should go to the station, they got plenty tucker there, plenty tucker. Jimmy Pike and

Above: Peter Skipper and a young friend in Fitzroy Crossing.

'Marawali, 1987', acrylic on linen, 183 x 122 cm.

'Jila Japingka I, 1989,' acrylic on linen, 213 x 137 cm.

me, we come to Cherrabun Station together. There was flour, white one, finish it up, sugar, big-mob sugar, fill up tea, stir it, finish it up... but we don't like sugar in tea, we just eat it by itself. We didn't know bullock, we come from desert country. When I first see bullock, I jumped in the river.

When I was walking around at Cherrabun Station and saw a bull (might be bullock). I ran straight up a tree, I'm frightened, I don't like big horn. One time I see a car coming up from the station. Then I jumped in the spinifex, 'cause the white man might see me. We didn't know, we were frightened. White man, he's different, he's got another colour, I got black colour, he's got white colour, he might take me to another place. He passes, he never saw me and I get up and walk. Jimmy Pike and me, we walk to the station, we're not frightened now. We started working there.

I work with horse and cattle, also the bore. The cattle drink water from a trough. I was frightened of the windmill, what is it doing? It gets the water with the wind, so I came out and looked at it. Then a plane comes along. I ran, ran, ran climbed up a tree. Inside in the airport, the plane lands, biggest plane. Picks up white man.

We go back to the desert again, come back up and down, I know now station and cattle. White man tells me: you gotta work here, I'll give you a job. I work on windmill, I make trough, I make fence, I do everything. I look after tanks – that's all white man's way. My mother and father, they teach me another way; they teach me to go out hunting for goanna. But white man taught me to make fence and build yard and windmill.

I worked in the bush away from the station, windmill job. I'm the windmill man. I ride horse, they showed me how. I mustered cattle, I clip their ears. Then I go along to another station, a sheep station. That's a different way. There I planted trees, wattle, everything.

Duncan, he sells my paintings, came and taught me painting. I get to Sydney and Adelaide. Duncan tells me you can draw alright. Duncan tells me you want to draw, if you want to draw I'll make you canvas. Alright he gives me canvas and paint, black and red and white, I paint. I tell him my story, this my story from desert. Alright next time he makes me a big canvas, I paint my sandhill, living water, soak water.

I put down the story from early days. I paint every morning and every afternoon I paint, I paint about the stories from early days, from what happened walking around with the early-days people. My story comes from the desert not from the station. I paint from my mother and father and grandfather and grandmother, in the desert always, I don't paint from the station, no, that's the way I draw, I draw my country.

Note: Duncan Kentish acts as an agent for Peter Skipper.

MERRILEE LANDS:
Author and Publicist

Merrilee Lands, as well as being an author in her own right, works as the Information and Promotions Officer for Magabala Books — an Aboriginal-controlled publishing house based in Broome, Western Australia. Magabala is the word used in many Aboriginal languages in the Kimberley area for the bush banana which, when dry, disperses seeds that travel a long way in the wind.

The publishing project was set up in 1987 by the Kimberley Aboriginal Law and Culture Centre. Magabala's editorial charter includes publishing stories and oral histories from the Kimberley and providing outlets for Aboriginal authors all over Australia.

The publications to date include Wandering Girl *by Glenyse Ward,* Raparapa *edited by Paul Marshall,* Story About Feeling *by Bill Neidjie,* Lori *by John Wilson,* Mayi – Some Bush Fruits of Dampierland *by Merrilee Lands,* The Story of Crow, *by Pat Torres and Magdalene Williams and* Jalygurr-Aussie Animal Rhymes *by Pat Torres and* Jilji – Life In The Great Sandy Desert *by Pat Lowe and Jimmy Pike.*

Magabala was set up as a result of a meeting held at Nguman in the Kimberley, when people from all over the region met at the Kimberley Law and Culture Centre. They met to voice their concern that a lot of the traditional aspects of Aboriginal language and living weren't being preserved, basically because of the breakdown of the oral tradition. No longer are our young people sitting down with elders. For those of us living in towns, there's no camp-fire business going on anymore, oral material isn't being passed down like it was for generations and generations. So our people wanted to see this traditional material being preserved and being made available for kids in the future.

One of the other reasons for Magabala being set up was that people were a bit worried that for a long time linguists and anthropologists were coming into the community and collecting stories and taking them away and that no-one ever knew what was happening to them. The Aboriginal people had no control over the material they had given, sometimes the material was published, yet they weren't going to get royalties. Magabala was set up with those two aims in mind – to preserve Aboriginal language and culture and to teach Aboriginal people about copyright.

Merrilee Lands and her daughter.

We're here essentially to serve Aboriginal people and we basically assess their work with our objectives in mind. Take Glenyse Ward's *Wandering Girl*. We published this book not just because it's written by an Aboriginal author (publishing Aboriginal authors is what we were set up to do) but also because it tells a history — a *hidden* history, one that a large proportion of the white Australian public didn't know about. What we consider when deciding to publish is, what good is the book going to do if we do publish it? And then we make the basic, normal publishing decision: like how expensive is the book going to be, how are we going to distribute it? And so on. We're here principally to produce books where Aboriginal people write their own personal histories and stories and put their point of view across. A lot of the things we know the white Australian public just don't know about. A lot of the histories that our people have witnessed or have been part of — especially the old people, with all those different laws that they had to live by, the citizenship rights debate and so on — these histories now can be put down for the sake of our people and also to make the wider public more aware. In this way we'll be able to get into the mainstream.

Since the Bicentennial year there's been a sudden swing towards Aboriginal issues and it's really brought us up into the limelight. With that recognition now we can go ahead and make sure that things are done right. A lot of white people are ignorant, they just don't know the sort of things that happened to our people. Being able to educate and inform them about certain issues will make them think differently: it will give them something to think about and it will ensure they are informed before making judgments on things they know nothing about.

Two of our children's books by Pat Torres — *Jalygurr-Aussie Animal Rhymes* and *The Story of Crow* — are bilingual books and contain two languages which are supposedly dead: the Yawuru language from Broome (there are only about fourteen speakers of Yawuru left) and then the Nyul Nyul language from the Beagle Bay area. All our books have got Aboriginal language throughout: *Mayi — Some Bush Fruits of Dampier Land* gave fruits spoken in five different languages spoken in the Dampier region. And then in *Raparapa* each of the storytellers — there were nine altogether, nine stockmen — gives a different bush name for everything.

This is a great project because now that our history is being recorded our kids are going to have those books to look at when we're dead and gone, at least they'll have something to fall back on. A lot of the material has already been lost. Every day it's being lost as an elder dies and takes all his knowledge with him. A lot of us haven't lived traditional lives — but there *is* a move, with people like Pat Torres and myself, to go back and learn traditional things, to want to learn the language, to try to get back into the traditional law and to push the kids to it as well. All of this has been neglected. It's only now that we're realising how important our traditional background — our Aboriginal background — is and that nothing much has been done about recording it.

For so long the previous generation was told forget it, forget it, forget it ... and they're still in that frame of mind. Now it's our generation that's going in there and telling them, "What you know is important, remember it, don't try to hide it, don't try to take it away with you, tell us, tell us."

It's an exciting time we're living in. Things have changed. At school we didn't really want to know about our own oral history because we were called names and things. This persists in our everyday attitude: in our mind we think we've got to be better and that that's to be like the Europeans — we've got to dress like them, we've got to be accepted... Every day you still feel it, you still feel you're not accepted and you *want* to be accepted, I don't know why. I was brought up in a mission. My mum was taken away from her parents and put into an orphanage and then she went out to work for somebody on a station and then they had a blue and so she ended up on a mission. My mother and I lived in dormitories. Then I went down to school in the city... Maybe the feeling comes from that, I don't know.

I don't know if you ever get rid of it — as far as I'm concerned it will always be in my mind. The damage done to me is permanent. I don't know when I'll ever get out of that frame of thinking of wanting to be accepted. I always feel I'm not equal. This feeling will always be there in me: never mind what you do, no matter what you do, how hard you try, you'll always have someone come along and just kill your determination, kill your confidence. That's one of the reasons why bringing our kids up differently — you know, with the right way of thinking — is so important because it determines how they turn out.

That's also one of the reasons why Magabala is so important. There's a big need to get Aboriginal curriculums going in schools; the kids have no Aboriginal material, you know. They *need* Aboriginal books, they're crying out for them — whatever they can get their hands on.

We've got a few projects going for schools. We've got a "Yawuru Seasons Kit" which tells you what foods are available at what time, what animals are fat in what seasons and when to leave all the skinny things alone, also what fish is on the run. This kit gives information in both traditional-language names *and* scientific names. At the school here the teachers take the kids out on field trips so they can see what's available for themselves and become familiar with all that kind of stuff.

The kit is just in the Yawuru language. The idea is that other schools which have another language can change all the words into their own language; so it can be used everywhere, even by European kids.

Information is one-sided at the moment. People only see bad things, because it's usually only the negative parts of Aboriginal people that are exposed to them. If you show them the positive side then that's when you change their thinking. And that's where school comes in. If European kids are fascinated by the Aboriginal topics they're taught at school, then they'll be making the Aboriginal kids proud. It makes so much more sense for our schools to use traditional Aboriginal material — all kids in Australia are familiar with the kangaroo and the emu, so why are they listening to stories like "Jack and Jill went up the hill" and "Humpty Dumpty sat on the wall"? Kids can't really relate to those nursery rhymes — it's only when they read about those things that they see around them that they relate to them. At the moment they learn very little about their own place . . .

MUDROOROO NAROGIN:
Writer

Mudrooroo Narogin (previously Colin Johnson) was born in Narrogin, Western Australia in 1938. Initially educated in an orphanage, he later found himself on the streets of Melbourne. After his first publication Wild Cat Falling *he travelled in Asia, in the US and in the UK and spent seven years of his life as a Buddhist monk.*

On returning to Australia he joined the Aboriginal Research Unit at Monash University in Melbourne. In 1979 he wrote Long Live Sandawara. *In 1980 he co-authored (with Colin Bourke and Isobel White)* Before the Invasion: Aboriginal Life to 1788. *In 1983 Hyland House published his third novel,* Doctor Wooreddy's Prescription For Enduring The Ending Of The World *and in 1986 Hyland House also published* The Song Circle of Jacky and Selected Poems. *His latest book is a critical look at the development of Aboriginal writing entitled* Writing from the Fringe *also published by Hyland House. Mudrooroo Narogin is currently living and working in Caraki, New South Wales.*

I was born in Narrogin WA — hence my name. In 1988 I decided that to have an English name wasn't very appropriate. Seeing as I was born in a little place outside Narrogin called East Coballing, which is only a post office and not much else, and since Narrogin was the name on my birth certificate I decided I would use "Narogin" at least as my nom-de-plume. "Mudrooroo" came about because I was talking to Oodgeroo Noonuccal in 1988 and she, in the course of discussion, said that we should have a working totem or dreaming. Then she said seeing that we are writers why not the paperbark tree? "Oodgeroo" means paperbark in the Noonuccal language and "Mudrooroo" means paperbark in the Bibbulmum language which is my mother's people's language; and so I changed my name to Mudrooroo. Now that evolved into "Mudrooroo Nyungar" which is my people's name. I then became tired of explaining what Nyungar meant. (The term "Aboriginal" or "Aborigine" is a white imposition on the indigenous peoples of Australia; being a Nyungar means something different to being an "Aboriginal" — we're a mix of races who belong to the south-west of Western Australia.) So my name now is Mudrooroo Nyungar and my nom-de-plume is still Narogin.

I've always been aware of my black heritage. This awareness came

A BICENTENNIAL GIFT POEM

I wish to remember the secret word dreamt at my initiation. I wish to feel again the burning of that burning yet again. I want the storm to renew my childhood. I want the river to return my canoe and the blue-skinned crabs from which I sucked the white meat from the claws of my undoing. I want to be more than a twitch in King Willy's arm. I want to say YES to the very leaf which aims its touch at my head making my totem tremble in some hidden space men know and keep alight until the time comes to be soaked in the sodden downpour streaking the red with the deadly white phantoms arriving to mingle with the Nyungar people while mouthing out platitudes of awful spite in too many messages containing the promises of brickbats on King Willy's forehead.

— **MUDROOROO NAROGIN**
Unpublished

from my mother: the Bibbulmum people are matrilineal so the female line is very very important to us. It was from my mother that I got most of my culture and also most of my complexes — one of the latter was not being white. When we went to the primary school in Beverley, lo and behold, what did we find but that it was segregated: all the black kids had to sit in a certain area of the room separated from the white kids. Naturally we rebelled against that, so we started wagging school and all the rest of it. You were always discriminated against if you lived in a country town; and if you're an Aboriginal then you're discriminated against since the time you were born. This discrimination becomes part of your psyche.

In Beverley where I grew up we had a house which was quite important; I went into that in *Wild Cat Falling*. A lot of Aboriginal people of course didn't have a house. This was a very social separation: if you *did* have a house you were supposed to conform to white dictates; and then of course because of the policies at the time, you lived in terror of being taken away from your parents. This is exactly what happened to my brothers and sisters and eventually what happened to me. It's what we call the "stolen generation." The whole policy, even up to now, is evident when I go home to Western Australia: most of the Nyungar people I know have had that experience of being taken away from their parents and put into homes. This has led to a breakdown in Nyungar families — yet we have all this propaganda about how Nyungar families have extended families and how Nyungar people look after each other. In a lot of cases it isn't like that — and this is because people like myself, as children, were taken away and put into orphanages and homes. The way we were graded was by skin colour. If you were light enough like me you went in to a place like Clontarf which was a Catholic boys' school; if you were darker you were sent to New-Norcia, which is a Catholic place for darker boys.

I was about eight or nine when I was taken away. What happened was that local farmers used to come into town on weekends and order their supplies which would be put outside the stores; sometimes, if they got drunk enough they'd forget their supplies and go home. So, if you got up early on Sunday morning you could go around and have such luxuries as bananas and fruits and so on. Eventually we — my sister and myself — were caught helping ourselves to these luxuries; we went before a magistrate and were sent to institutions in Perth.

Later in life I travelled for a while. I decided to go overland to Europe and was struck by Thailand at the time, where white people are in the minority. I saw Buddhist monks in Thailand and was invited into a temple to stay. It was peaceful, I felt very free for some reason in Thailand and also in India. So I became a monk for seven years in India. I wouldn't be a monk now but I'm still a Buddhist. Traditional Aboriginal chanting is very, very similar to Buddhist chanting. There are other interesting links — such as the emphasis on law. The law in India is Dharma, which is a Sanskrit concept. In Aboriginal culture the law is an impersonal force but it's what governs all of life, you can't dispute it; it's the same in Buddhism. In both cases the law is there and it's impersonal, it's not based on any high deity or anything like that. This is how I can relate to the law in Buddhism and the law in Aboriginal thought.

What I like about Aboriginal thought especially is the value of dreaming. Dreaming is the field of creation. So it's here that you can develop a true Aboriginal literature rather than just sitting down and telling the story — "Hey this is the truth, man, this is what they done to us," or something like that. Actually I don't think youth is angry anymore, it's been sort of brainwashed and manipulated. My novel *Long Live Sandawara* was written in 1974 when youth was considered to have some revolutionary fervour, or else to have some power. Since *Long Live Sandawara* the whole youth issue has been wiped out, youth has been rendered powerless.

I would exclude, to a certain extent, black youth or Aboriginal youth in Australia. *They,* more or less, have a tradition to go back to. White youth in Australia haven't anything except surfing, they are very non-culture... Australia is very interesting in that way: it's very thin the Australian culture, you can sort of poke your finger through to the vacuum on the other side and so it's a very nihilistic and a very hedonistic and very much a suffering society. Youth suffer in Australian society a lot, they haven't been given very much scope to develop. You can't really base life on just a material level, yet it is happening not only to youth but to the mature human beings as well. All they have is work, children, the home, material possessions and nothing else — so it's not rich enough, it's not a rich enough mix and so people suffer.

I wanted to write Australia's first Beatnik novel, its first existentialist novel — I think I succeeded in *Wild Cat Falling* in doing precisely that. I say I succeeded because I find that book still relevant today, I still believe in a lot of the things I wrote in it. We shouldn't be so concerned with exposing the crimes of the Europeans anymore, it just becomes tedious. There's lots of problems with this of course: the novel as a means of getting anything across is supposedly dead at the moment — but as long as they're produced you should try to develop some sort of style to handle material instead of just being a reporter and writing it out. But unfortunately all we're getting at the moment is the reportage... which can be pretty bloody dreary.

What I'm more concerned about is (say) for example to show Aboriginal humour. Humour in Aboriginal culture is very very strong. (I think there's a Marxist analysis in there somewhere: humour is a result of being oppressed, isn't it? All oppressed people have as a weapon *is* humour.) But a lot of people don't like the Aboriginal sense of humour which can be very cruel; still, though, it is part of Aboriginal culture. To have a humour is to have a style. What I liked about *Coordah,* Richard Walley's first play, is that he has the Aboriginal trickster-character in it. I really like that, because the trickster-character is in lots of cultures and it's very strong in Aboriginal culture too.

I haven't found much development in the novel. As I wrote in my book *Writing from the Fringe* we should get into Aboriginal reality, which is the Dreaming *now.* But what happens is that there's too many plays and stories in which the reality is very flat and is only "what they done to us". As I said, I find this exceedingly tedious. I have a big problem with this sort of realism. Aboriginal reality is more akin to surrealism in fact, because it's based on the Dreaming — the "dreaming" we did when we had really dynamic traditional culture. When I hear the traditional stories and when I read them I find them a lot more interesting than a lot of the Aboriginal literature being produced now. So I think that in order to create a dynamic Aboriginal literature we have to go back to the very roots of Aboriginal culture, to traditional Aboriginal culture. I feel this is the way to go — that we should be developing our own literature and not just utilising Australian realism... which I don't like as a literary medium anyway.

I don't think Aboriginal theatre has developed much, to tell you the truth. I think *The Cake Man* by Bob Merrit and *The Cherry Pickers* by Kevin Gilbert, more or less set the scene; Jack Davis has also established his sort of realist-type theatre. Usually to have theatre anywhere in Australia you have to have the kind of theatre conditioned by white preoccupations, and so this is what you more or less get with Aboriginal theatre. Now I don't actually know exactly how Aboriginal theatre should be handled. Possibly it can be done as Jack Davis did in *Dreamers,* which was quite good and had a complex time-structure. But, when you come to *No Sugar* that element begins to disappear and the same applies for *Barungin (Smell the Wind),* which is really just straightforward realism. I don't see it as a failing — I just see it as a phase, possibly not a very good phase... It also depends on what theatre is; does one *need* theatre? Theatre is a very *bourgeois* art form unfortunately.

My favourite books would be *Fringedweller,* by Robert Bropho, *A Story About Feeling* by Big Bill Neidje and *Gularubulu* by Paddy Roe. This is how I would like to see Aboriginal literature develop instead of just having a straight, linear plot...

PAT TORRES:
Storyteller and Writer

Pat Torres is based in Broome, Western Australia and lives with her four young children. She graduated from university with a BA degree and a Diploma of Education. She has spent several years collecting stories and other information from the Yawuru and Nyul Nyul tribal elders in their own language. Pat has been using this data to produce several children's books which comprise elements of traditional languages. She uses imaginative illustrations to portray the animals and activities that figure in her stories. Thus The Story of Crow, *her second book features both the Nyul Nyul language and* Jalygurr-Aussie Animal Rhymes *features the Yawuru language. Both are published by the Aboriginal publishing house* Magabala.

When I was about eighteen and studying anthropology and linguistics I started thinking about who I was, where I was going and where I came from. In those days — that's from the early to the mid-1970s — the concept of Aboriginality was only just starting to emerge and even to call yourself an Aboriginal in a small country town was still a very political thing. That, and the European culture around me, meant I had never really known how I should identify myself. I'd just tried to be a person in Australian society, to just get on and be a human being in this world, on this planet . . . but nobody wanted to accept me as that. They were stereotyping me all the time whenever I went for a job, or to the bank or something like that, they were always stereotyping me as being Aboriginal, Aboriginal, all the time . . . I realised I'd have to decide what I was. Intuitively I knew who I was, I was also aware of the negative conditioning that was happening to me. At that point I decided that I *was* Aboriginal and that I came from the Yawuru people in Broome. I also decided that from then on I'd work for the betterment of Aboriginal people — my *own* people.

I went to Tasmania and started to work with the Tasmanian Aboriginal Centre on a special project: a socioeconomic survey of the households in Tasmania. I was surprised to find there were 14 000 Aboriginal descendants living in Tasmania — descendants of the original Tasmanian people. We had to deal with this total myth about all Aboriginal people being dead in Tasmania. I used to have to visit schools and give talks about the fact that there were Tasmanian Aboriginal people who *did* exist and who were very much alive — real people, not ghosts and spirits walking around . . .

They were good years, those years I spent in Tasmania, but they were also traumatic — having to cope all the time with people who kept denying that Aboriginals existed. It gave me good reason for coming home really. When I got back here I started trying to find out more about my own roots, to go really deep. You know. . . I knew a lot of traditional stories; but trying to write them down and record them, was another thing altogether.

That was what formed the basis of my children's stories: once I started collecting information about my family and my history all the Dreamtime stories started coming out, oral histories recalling World War II and of how Aboriginal people used to be treated by Europeans in the old days. I thought I was really lucky to be given all this information about our culture and our history and our languages; I thought our culture is *alive*, it's not dead, so I must try and preserve it in some way because the oral history tradition is being hampered by the way we live today. Nowadays we don't live around a camp-fire where you can just sit down and listen to stories regularly and learn about your country and your land; instead we work from nine to five and we send our children to a State education system or a Catholic education system. So one way I thought I could assist my own people was to write all this information down for future generations and for my own children. I wanted them to realise who they are and where they come from so they won't have to cope with some of the things *I* had to cope with when I was growing up because they'd have all the information there.

Take the history of our town: here people of half-caste inheritance were removed from their families and placed into orphanages, so as to be "re-educated". My own mother was a victim of that. We had something like ten other races here mixing with Aboriginal people. Most of the children from those relationships — depending on how black they were — were herded into institutions, sometimes physically removed, and there was even a time when the Welfare Department used to go and kidnap children from their mothers. (They'd claim that the mothers were unfit, that they were taking the children — which was legally permitted by the Government — because what they were trying to do was to save the race by educating the children!) My grandmother and my mother were removed from their families and educated to be house servants for station owners — white families.

You know, it was only the half-caste ones that they took away to do that. In many cases those young children got taken to places and made to work for wealthy European pioneers as their servants; basically they were unpaid — just given food and clothing and shelter. Glenyse Ward tells the story of how she, even in her generation, went through that same system, how she was used as a very cheap slave by the family she lived with. That sort of thing was really rife in this country up here. The Government was trying to "re-educate" the Aboriginal people to become worthy citizens of Australia...

There are many people who grew up in the Beagle Bay Mission system and much of the language and culture from that area has completely died out. The missionaries denied the cultural practices of the Nyul Nyul-speaking people, they actually forbade our law. They placed the European God into our traditional belief system and said that this was the new God, they actually stopped our law and traditional practices from happening and just superimposed Christianity in their place. Whenever missionaries herded young Aboriginal children into an orphanage and found them speaking their language to each other then they were flogged, bashed, punished severely in one way or another. When a generation has grown up like that they've generally lost contact with their language and their culture. Luckily in Beagle Bay there was one old man who was a renegade: he'd sneak back and talk to the kids across the fence and kept contact with them in this way. As a result there are still people who can speak the Nyul Nyul language, because after seeing what the old man had done more people sneaked back to talk to their kids through the fence at night. They'd sneak back and do their corroborees and ceremonies. So bits and pieces of our language and law *have* been preserved, we *still* have people around who can give it back to us.

I believe the time has come for us Aboriginal people to be creative, to redevelop our artistic talents, to share those artistic talents at whatever level they occur: art, and song, and dance and plays are just some of the many different mediums you can use to convey important information about Aboriginal culture.

Some of these legendary animals are being drawn for the first time; people have never seen them before, they've just been stories. So when I'm trying to draw a gumbun — a gumbun is a spiritual being that lives in the mangrove, it's half like an ape but it's also a spiritual being — I'm trying to draw something like that for the first time. And it's really hard.

I hope to portray these beings — and our belief about them — in a contemporary fashion because now we live in a world where we have to learn how to read and write. Our old people are rapidly dying and the information we have is dying with them, so we have to get hold of it and put it into new formats like books, films and tapes which will preserve it for the future. We never abused the land like it's being abused now and hopefully if people can listen and learn some of the truths we have learnt about how to survive and live in the land then they may have a better world to live in for themselves too.

When I do my paintings I look for the designs specific to my area. Aboriginal people should seek designs that are specific to their own culture and recreate their own information using their traditional knowledge. Aboriginal culture in Australia in the past has been really diverse and still is today. We've gone through incredible changes since the coming of white people to this country but we went through changes long before that too. We still survive because we are adaptable. Our skin might change but our spirit doesn't. Today we use an axe made out of steel or we hunt with a gun if we want a kangaroo or something like that. We use a Landrover to catch our food — but what we're doing is we're just adapting the tools, you see. We're adapting the tools to carve out the life we seek, we still go and get our bush food, we still go and get our bush medicines . . . but instead of using axes and spears now we're using the tools of white people, the tools that white people have provided. White people aren't using the tools that *they* came out of the cave with either! All societies throughout the world have adapted and changed.

By educating people about our history and our culture and where we're coming from we gain a greater understanding and awareness of other peoples' cultures and belief systems — why we do what we do and why we think what we think. This leads, I guess, to a better world.

RICHARD WALLEY:
Director and Playwright

Richard Walley is an experienced and highly respected theatre director, actor, playwright, musician, dancer and choreographer.

He founded, with Ernie Dingo and others, the Middar Aboriginal Theatre in Western Australia. Both with the company and independently, he has toured to numerous international events and festivals, and indeed, has been recognised and appreciated overseas far more widely than in his own country.

Richard's stage appearances include productions (by Western Australian theatre companies), of A Fortunate Life, The Dreamers *and* No Sugar, *which toured to the 1987 World Expo theatre in Canada. He has also worked as assistant director on Jack Davis' plays on several occasions; he has worked on radio and television in the UK, USA, Canada and Denmark; he has appeared in the television series of* A Fortunate Life.

His plays include Coordah, *and recently* Munjong *which opened at the Victorian Arts Centre in Melbourne in March 1990. Richard currently lives in Perth, and continues to travel widely because of his work.*

I went to a convent school. I was the only Aboriginal in the whole school, and I copped all the racist jokes and blame for everything that went wrong there, which led me to have quite a negative approach to white society for a number of years. I used it to motivate myself in such a way that anything I wanted to do I'd make sure I'd do it better than any white person, because we *had* to do it better. If it wasn't done better it wasn't accepted.

I went to work as an apprentice boilermaker/welder in the Australian iron and steel industry for the next eight or nine years, and then I went into the Aboriginal political arena where for five years I chaired the Aboriginal Advisory and the Aboriginal Consultative Committee. I was heavily involved in sports and black politics. I got into Aboriginal music and started playing the didgeridoo. I formed a group called Middar Aboriginal Theatre with several others. As the group found itself more and more in demand I went into acting and started appearing in plays.

The first thing I found was that the roles were very very stereotyped and that a white writer could not write the words as an Aboriginal person would say them. I was continually changing a lot of the writing around and speaking to writers who knew nothing about Aboriginals or how they

COORDAH

Lights come up on two Aborigines sharing a bottle next to a log amid bush. One of the men is NUMMY, *known as the local drunk. The other is mentally retarded. He is* GINNA.

GINNA: But Elly said I not to drink.
NUMMY: Sip it. You're not drinking then — just sipping.
GINNA: Yeh — and den what you done?
NUMMY: Well, after about a hour I said to them *wetjalas*, 'Put your guns away. I'll show youse how to catch a 'roo'. None of them white fellas knew how to shoot! Anyway, they laughed at me and said 'OK, smart arse — show us what you can do!' So I picked up two stones and walked toward the creek and they followed me. At the bottom of the creek was this big boomer. Must have been about, or between five or seven feet tall.
GINNA: And you killed him?
NUMMY: No. He was too big. Them big ones no good — too tough. No. I stayed behind the bush and told the *wetjalas* to be still and quiet . . . then soon, a smaller one hopped along. When he reached the water . . .
GINNA: You shot him.
NUMMY: No. I just whistled and the 'roos stood up looking around. Then I threw one of the stones, high up in the air and they looked up watching it. They didn't want it to land on their head. Then I threw the other stone and hit the 'roo fair in the head — killing him stone dead.
GINNA: The big one.
NUMMY: No, the middle-sized one.
GINNA: What middle-size one?
NUMMY: Oh, he hopped in when the stone was in the air and looked up.
GINNA: You musta thrown the stone a long way up.
NUMMY: Yeh. I hit a duck too. It was flying past at the same time.
   [NUMMY's *story is interrupted by* TREB, *who enters carrying a guitar.* TREB *is* NUMMY's *brother-in-law and* GINNA's *brother.*]
TREB: What are you two up to?
GINNA: Hey, my brother.
NUMMY: Treb. We just yarning.
GINNA: Yeh, boy. Just yarning.
TREB: You blokes not drinking?
NUMMY: No.
GINNA: No. We just sipping.
TREB: Ginna. You know Elly will flog you if you go home with just a smell of drink on you!
   [GINNA *bows his head.*]
   Did you save me a charge?
   [NUMMY *hands* TREB *the bottle. He takes a drink and shakes his head.*]
   Where did you get this *gebba* from?
NUMMY: It's home made — old Tony. Only eighty cents a bottle.
TREB: Phoo! It's rotten stuff.
   [*He drinks some more.*]
NUMMY: Well. Let's do some real rehearsing.
   [NUMMY *pulls out another bottle as* TREB *strums his old guitar.* GINNA *just smiles.*]

— **RICHARD WALLEY**

should write. So I thought I may as well write things myself. Jack Davis had told me to write. (I'd worked with Thomas Keneally on his play called *Bullies House* in the US. Thomas had also said, "Write".)

Jack showed me more or less how to structure a play. The two plays I've written, *Coordah* and *Munjong*, were both very well received. In those plays I found a happy medium to present my kind of work. I'm pulling two worlds together — the Aboriginal and the white world — I'm communicating with both and I have to do justice to both without insulting one or the other.

Theatre is an area where you can educate as well as entertain. People don't want to be preached at. You must have a time in theatre when you can make them cry and make them laugh, that's why it's important to show the happy parts of Aboriginal life. So I've been taking all our bits of art and putting them into a very well-polished, well-rehearsed performance — either on stage, through radio, through television, film or whatever medium I can use, so as to educate not only non-Aboriginal Australians but also Aboriginal Australians. If we want to achieve something we have to really pursue it: no-one is going to hand you things on a platter; and the harder we work the more we're going to achieve. Nothing has been given to us, in fact most things have been taken away from us. It's because of that sort of experience that Aboriginal artists have been combining to help each other... and we've had a great combination and collaboration and cooperation between Aboriginal artists.

The first theatre that ever took place in Australia was Aboriginal theatre. Our corroborees are theatre, our storytelling is theatre. It's only lately that we've begun working in cooperation with white mainstream theatre. Theatre can be used in any form, any shape, by any person using any language, with any story, on any platform... Fundamentally there's a lot of difference in black and white theatre. You can stand erect on stage, you can do all the things which do not look natural and deliver a great performance as an actor — or else you can be a person who's not playing a role but *living* that piece of theatre. Not portraying your role as an actor but using it as a vehicle to describe what's been happening to people gone before you, to your people, to your life... that's what I think Aboriginal theatre is all about. I think that's the difference between mainstream theatre and our theatre.

What we really have to do is get the whole nation to support us as a national treasure rather than turn us into a political football or else turn us away as something second-rate. Whether Australians like it or not, every time we perform (either here or on an international platform) we're representing every Australian as well. Our culture *is* Australia's culture; the only culture in Australia *is* Aboriginal culture — everything else is a second-rate import.

Change is happening and it is happening simply because we're writing the material. The other generation did not have black playwrights. But we have our first black playwright still alive today, we have our first black poet still alive today, we have our first black novelist still alive today... so we're really new at all this and yet we've already made progress. We're learning how to use white language and literature so that now we're getting through to the masses. We've learnt their language and we're delivering messages to them in their language. I think the next generation will do this even better, we're going to have our own black movie directors and our own black television writers and our own black camera operators... We've come a long way in the last few years but we've still got a long way to go.

A lot of the arts are being used to look at Australia's history. History, whether people like it or not, is always the interpretation of some writers. You can have three different writers all describe the one event in their own individual, different ways. So, if you've got an oral history — like we have — then this means all of our written history has been done by anthropologists. So a lot of the history that was written about us was really a false history; and that's why Aboriginal people now have got to go back to the elders and put the true story down of what's really happened around here. Forget about hiding the shame and saying this should not have happened and this should not have occurred. It's just a matter of saying, these are the facts, this or that occurred and we want to write the facts, expose to Australia once and for all what's been going on. I think Australia will be a better country for it because once white Australians understand what's happened they will also understand why, in a lot of areas, there's been a lot of bitterness — a lot of bitterness for example between Aboriginals and police. This is the sort of history that we have to rewrite and say: this *has* happened, this *is* reality.

There is this change now with Aboriginal people saying we have to stop being negative and just be positive, but it's very very difficult when you've got front-page newspaper headlines about Aboriginal people still dying in custody. You can't turn your back and say, "Well that's not going to happen, we're not going to talk about that anymore, let's talk about something positive," because the reality is that we still have these problems.

We've only had that twenty-four years since we were recognised as citizens and given the vote, we are the first or maybe the second generation of people now who have the knowledge and the freedom to really express ourselves. Slowly, I think, we will get to the stage where we're getting less and less negative and more and more positive. We don't need sympathy, we need understanding — and the more we get people to understand us, the more they will accept us on our terms.

CENTRAL AUSTRALIA

Sun/Wanarringa design by Bede Tungutalum

BEDE TUNGUTALUM:
Designer and Artist

Bede Tungutalum and Giovanni Tipungwuti established Tiwi Designs at Nguiu on Bathurst Island in 1970. Since then Tiwi Designs has expanded so much that it now employs a significant proportion of the Tiwi population on Bathurst Island.

Tiwi designs are based on traditional stories as well as the fauna of Bathurst Island. Bede and Giovanni first transferred traditional images onto paper and then onto fabric using a silk screen. By using contemporary media they maintained links with their traditional culture while at the same time developing a viable financial organisation thereby encouraging economic autonomy for the Tiwi people.

Their designs are sold throughout Australia and overseas. In addition many art galleries, hotels and government offices in Australia hang their work. In 1985 Tiwi Designs was nominated for an International Design Award by the Japanese Design Foundation. Recently the company expanded into batik and poster-making.

After 20 years Bede has left the company, feeling that it is now time for him to pursue his own, individual artistic direction.

I left school in 1969 and I went to Darwin to study pottery. I worked there for nearly six months. I didn't like it, it wasn't very interesting, so I came back to the Island. We then had a teacher who taught us woodblock printing and who started me off on printing and making woodblock prints. Then in 1970, with help from the mission, me and Giovanni started a partnership, doing woodblock prints. Gradually we translated these into silk-screen prints.

In 1978 I was the art representative for the Commonwealth Games in Edmonton in Canada. We were there for a while. I looked at Indian art to see how they did prints on stones; they had quite a different way of doing it from us. That's where I got many of my first ideas from — from the Indians. In Vancouver they make very nice designs, and very good carvings as well. I actually visited some Indian Reservations and saw the people make their own carvings. Then in 1983 I went to Papua New Guinea for the South Pacific Arts Festival. Papua New Guinea is a nice place. People there they have their own culture — a very strong, very strong culture. I really like their carving. I got some ideas from them. I wouldn't mind going back there to study more.

74

Far Left: 'Shark', ochres and acrylic on black cotton, Bede Tungutalum. Left: Hand-painted T-shirt produced by Tiwi Designs. Above: Bowl, Jock Pauatjimi, Tiwi Designs.

We have a lot to learn from different indigenous arts. We should really see how different people work and what they are doing. They should come and learn our way as well. We should have a mixture of all the different cultures in the galleries — African, Indian, Maori, Aboriginal, Indonesian — their art is all quite different and there's a lot to learn from each other.

When Giovanni and me started off Tiwi Designs we just did single print designs in the beginning, like crabs, turtles, fish — all sorts of animals. The next year we started to form a company. Before it had been a partnership, not a company.

Tiwi Designs started in the new presbytery. We had about eight girls who did mostly the sewing, we did the printing and two old men did all the designs for us for the wall hangings. At that time, we mostly did wall hangings, table cloths and place mats. I taught a lot of the younger ones. We used to go to the school to see the kids and the ones who were very good in art. I would ask if they wanted to work at Tiwi Design.

Tiwi Designs was growing and growing and growing. Five years later we moved into another place, and I did bigger designs on fabric. I'm real happy with the development of Tiwi Designs. It's selling a lot overseas now. Some designs represent my life, like my Dreaming.

I've left the company now. I just want to start my own business, to be on my own. I've been there for long enough — almost twenty years. I just want to do something different. I do all different sorts of things now like carving, screen-printing, a little bit of woodblock printing, I love woodblock printing — I like painting a lot too.

The mission doesn't have a big influence here anymore. It's all run by the Tiwi Land Council. The Council runs the settlement. The only things the mission runs now is the school and hospital. We have our own housing association and our local people do the building. Local people go to Sydney for four years to do a training course in building. They then come back and run the Housing Association and build what we need.

Tiwi in my language means "people", it stands for "one people". Tiwi Designs was my dream to create something for the people. I set it up but now I want to break away to do something for myself. Twenty years is long enough. I'm thinking of sculpting in bronze. I was asked in Sydney last year to go back for six months and study bronze casting. I'd like that. I could do birds, all sorts of sculptures. I'd keep painting, just so I can relate to here, to the birds and animals.

GEOFFREY GORDON LINDSAY: *Artist*

Geoffrey Gordon Lindsay is from South Australia but currently lives in Perth, Western Australia. He has only recently started working as an artist and his images have a distinct, graphic quality, drawing both from traditional stories and incorporating traditional beliefs with an almost futuristic style.

He works in a broad spectrum of mediums including pencil, ink, acrylic, metal, lino, and makes jewellery.

I come from South Australia, a place called Gerard Mission near the fruit industry up around Barma and I was born 2 feet from the May River. My tribe is called Naringey. Apparently my skin name is Ponde which I've just recently started to use in my painting. I was taken away when I was about eighteen-months-old – something to do with not eating. I did have polio when I was twelve but I was only sent home when I was eighteen, so I didn't have much time with my parents and family. I've travelled around a lot; and every time I get a chance to get home, I go home. I was going to become a pilot but because of a head injury from an accident I had to start all over again: 1, 2, 3, square, circle, blue, yellow... I *still* have difficulty writing; I can read alright, but my spelling is awful – so I don't worry about it.

I've been painting for four, four-and-a-half years now. I became an artist late in life. When I was twenty-eight. I realised I had a bit of talent but I didn't really follow it up until I was in prison. At first, prison was fairly awful but you get used to any system. You *have* to get used to it in order to survive; and by using the elements around me I became much more powerful in the mind than I thought I could be. I think that really helped me to look at my future and reach a point where I could say, I can get out of here and do nothing or I can continue to develop my art. It's the worst place you can be, prison: if you can survive in that sort of atmosphere with a mind that is imaginative, if you can survive with *any* imagination whatsoever in prison and you can look at the day and say you had a good day and smile about it to yourself, then you've done alright.

I was first in prison in Broome and then they moved me down to Fremantle. It was in Broome that I started to realise I did have a talent at drawing, but I wasn't sure what direction I should go in. I finished up at Kenivale and I really got into art there. It wasn't a question of having to be

in a happy sort of a mood in order to be able to paint; that wasn't my story in jail because it is a place of frustrations, fear, anger, jealousy, spite — you name it, jail's got it... So I had to tap into all that pent-up energy instead — because that was what was there all the time. I had to get absolutely mean, frustrated and angry... Then my imagination becomes much stronger than if I were to think of something beautiful, happy and joyful. I used that for inspiration. I got myself angry; and when I got myself angry the power was there.

I do very graphic work. When I see something, I don't see it as visual. I have a mental approach to it. In jail I started to see things around me in a different perspective, so I drew things as I saw them — you could say I saw them for the first time. The things I express in my paintings are not necessarily to do with the cultural side of my life — it's more to do with my interpretation of certain stories I hear, or else of experiences that fascinate me, things from my own personal life even. For instance: painting a cup of water or even a cup of tea. It's not so much the cup of tea or what's in it, it's more, how does drinking tea make you feel? What's in the actual tea that makes you feel good when you drink it? That's the kind of thing I try to capture on paper. It's sometimes very difficult, there are so many ways you can express it but I try to describe not only the shape of the cup but also the feeling of refreshment, the feeling in you that makes you feel good after a nice cup of tea.

I still draw inspiration from things that anger me, like a dog barking at me. I walk along the street and I get a dirty look from someone that gives me energy, not that I have to go looking for that particular element. There's a lot of places these days where that kind of frustration — anger and jealousy — still exists in everyday life, but I don't have to put up with it every day. I've got a world I can creep into and be happy in myself.

I do more damage to myself the more intelligent I become, the more dangerous I am to myself. I would prefer to be... not dumb but *passive*, with a life that's easy and free. Now I have to know a lot more things than I did in the past so it's a lot harder even just in terms of expressing myself. It's a lot harder now, just living. I figure out ways of getting things I don't need in the first place, I become more cynical. It's like a multiple game, a circle that's never ending.

Today you can't survive living like an Aboriginal because you've got all these things against you and your culture. It's hard enough surviving in your own culture let alone a culture that doesn't want a part of you — even though you do your utmost to actually learn. There's just no way the

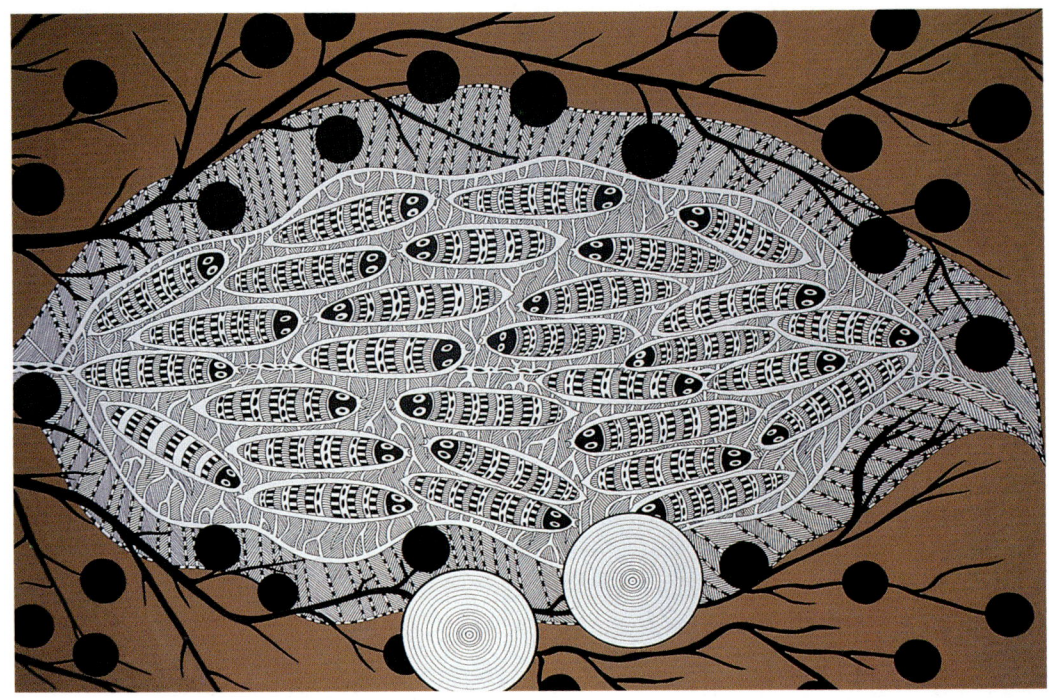

Top: 'The sounds of the Nullarbor'.
Above: Untitled.

Europeans will accept you as part of their culture. White culture is a very confusing culture; as far as I can make anything of it from the experience I've had in life, there's always a line, there's always prejudice in white culture. I feel that every time I succeed in doing something in their culture all hell breaks loose. As an artist, if you put me against a white artist, it is my culture that seems to be the main subject — it's the culture and not so much the painting I've just finished. I don't want to be called an Aboriginal painter, I want to be called an artist first and then an Aboriginal second. But I always seem to have to go the long way around things...

There's no quality in European culture, there's no peace within life itself, it's a struggle. And once you get up there, there is nowhere else to go. I can't see European culture as being something worth following. I still see the days when I was a kid, having a swim in the river, eating, fishing and sleeping and enjoying life, experiencing nature around me. My culture has a deeper feeling than Christianity.

So, where can you go? Do you have a home unit, become a big business man, have hundreds of dollars? Where is that going to get you? A better tie, a better pair of socks? I just can't figure it out: the more money I have, the less I think of myself and the more I spend it... and of course I don't spend it wisely.

I look at the news and I say, okay you run me and my race down — and then I laugh. So there's still my laughter. It's a joke, I could be from the lowest race on earth but at least I look at the news and I laugh...

ANDREW SPENCER JAPALJARRI:
Artist and Counsellor

Andrew Spencer Japaljarri is a Warlpiri from Yuendumu in the Northern Territory. He now lives in Alice Springs and is working with HALT — the Healthy Aboriginal Life Team. Andrew has produced several visual posters in a series which deals with current issues and problems in Aboriginal communities. In symbols used traditionally in body-painting, sand-drawing and permanent engravings on rock and wood Andrew produces new stories discussing new situations such as family breakdowns, petrol-sniffing, alcohol abuse and AIDS. This method of disseminating important information has since been adopted by a number of other indigenous workers at Yuendumu, Kintore, Kiwirrkura, Ernabella, Fregon, Indulkana, Alice Springs and Tennant Creek.

When I started working in my own community there was no grog. That's 1960 I'm talking about. The Europeans used to run the town like superintendents. There used to be no grog in the town, people used to work and on Friday afternoon they'd go out hunting and come back Sunday afternoon. In 1966 we had small roads first, now we've got big ones. Then people started travelling, in the 1970s, from Alice Springs to Yuendumu; this was when people started bringing grog into the community and started drinking. The place has been getting worse and worse and worse. From 1970 to 1990 it's been a big problem.

The problem with Aboriginal people only started when the grog came into the community. People started to think the grog is better, it makes you happy, it can't make you sad when your family pass away, it will take your pain away. That's why a lot of people who have lost their family, they want to drink, drink, drink and sort the problem out that way. In my opinion that's wrong. We should sit down and try and talk to the family about what problems they've got. Otherwise the grog will kill them. In our community when people pass away there's a lot of family to take over, so we want to get rid of this grog in the town. We've got to look at the future. We are talking about Aboriginal history, about the future...

Some of my posters and paintings talk about petrol-sniffing. When people come in from other areas — say a family comes for a ceremony or

'Family breakdown' a poster produced by HALT (Healthy Aboriginal Life Team).

something like that — the kids start running around. And when they see one kid sniffing they ask, "What's that?" The kid then says, "That's petrol, you can sniff it." So they try it; that's how it keeps going, that's how it spreads. In some areas there are no sniffers because they've got a strong community and they have helpers. Where the red dots are, that's where they've got weak communities: but people can stop the petrol-sniffing there through family control. They say petrol is like grog, but it's *not* like grog: petrol can kill your kids. We had some kids pass away in 1983. Petrol can paralyse you, some kids couldn't walk.

We used to grow up in a family but now people go their separate ways, that's what our family breakdown is about. Brothers, sisters, mothers, fathers, grandfathers... they all go their different ways and the kids get into trouble, worse and worse trouble, then they go to jail or pass away. How do we get the family back? We go and talk to a kid and find out where the rest of the family is, we look at all of the history of that family — not just the history of the mother and father but also of the uncle, aunt, the whole family — and then we think, where's that kid going to go? He goes to a strong family then. We've got surnames from Europeans, but in our culture we have skin names, we have ceremonies, we have our Dreaming and we follow our families. So if my son has some problems there's a family I can send him to — not only his mother.

In Aboriginal communities we've always waited for the Europeans to do things. Now we have to do these things ourselves and look to the future. How are we going to fix these problems? With our posters and paintings we travel not only through our own area but also in Queensland and other places. People understand our paintings just like it is a desert painting, or a Dreaming. Up here we use these paintings specially for the very young and for the old people, those who can't read.

These posters and paintings are not just for my people but for white people too. *They* might find something from us that they can turn around and use themselves. We are trying to work together with white people on these problems. Sometimes the white people want to do it themselves same as Aboriginal people but I don't want to see it like that, I want to work together with them for the future. Some think the white people have different problems; no, they're not different problems, they're the same problems but white people act in different ways. We want to see *all* people working together — that's the way I want to go. There's only one way to go — to work together to solve all these problems.

BANDUK MARIKA: *Artist*

Banduk Marika was born at Yirrkala Mission in north-east Arnhem Land in 1954. She left for Darwin when she was eighteen and in 1979 moved to Sydney, where she began to transfer some of the many drawings she had done onto lino. Since then she has had numerous exhibitions. She has been artist-in-residence at Flinders University, at the Canberra College of the Arts and at the Australian National Gallery. She is now a member of the Council at the National Gallery and so plays an important role in the selection of the Gallery's collection. She has also worked as an actress and film adviser on Aboriginal culture.

Her work is based on traditional stories from the Yirrkala region. Banduk is concerned that more art gets back to and is shown in the local Aboriginal communities. She managed the Buku Larnggay Local Art Centre and Museum. Banduk has now returned to live in Yirrkala but travels regularly for council meetings at the National Gallery.

I'm from Yirrkala, 500 miles north-east of Darwin. Home is right on the tip of the Gulf of Carpentaria, on the point before it drops into the gulf. Forest, monsoon land — always green — right on the ocean, beautiful sunsets, colour-changes in the sea and sky and clouds...

I was born and grew up there. A lot of my upbringing was traditional until the 1960s when I remember attending school. My family stopped moving about then; until then we were nomadic, moving around areas defined within traditional family boundaries. Melenboi used to be my family's traditional hunting grounds; it's a wild honey site. August, September would be time for geese, water chestnuts, water lilies, certain mullets coming up to breed, certain fish coming up to breed. But now, since the town was built there, the people rarely hunt. I remember my grandmothers would just take a few dilly bags carrying necessary things like maps, my father would carry spears and boomerangs. We travelled in dugout canoes, we camped, we covered a lot of territory.

Things changed with the missions; their main ideas was to bring the different clan-groups into a small space which they didn't share before. That didn't work well for a lot of people: some clan-groups might have had traditional differences — and bringing them together created conflict. People started marrying people they wouldn't have normally married, traditional marriages started breaking down.

I was brought up by two mothers anyhow. We don't see any difference

Baru, Marna, Ga Buthurumirri, lino print.

'Turtle Hunting at Bremer Island', lino print.

between mothers and cousins — we're all one and brought up as one. Those relations were the sorts of things being taken out of the culture. Traditional healing methods too were taken out of the culture; also the white people tried to break the language down — but that didn't succeed. There were a lot of things that were bad... but there were a lot of good things too — for instance, education. I wouldn't be here if I hadn't had an education. There were good things on the one hand and bad things on the other.

I came down to live in Sydney in late 1979, I was out at Fairfield West through to late 1983. I used to do drawings, I suppose it was a way of passing time. Sometimes you feel lonely when you're away from home, sometimes you need to do something to keep in touch somehow. That's why I did the drawings. Then I showed some to Jenny Issacs who suggested making them into prints.

When I started off I was just translating my father's work — which was traditional work — onto contemporary media. When I was a child and people were buying his work they'd see my work and say, "Oh you can't do that, you have to stick with bark painting." But bark painting wasn't traditional anyhow; Aboriginal people didn't paint on bark, it was the missions' idea of transferring the art to sell them. I'm doing the same thing now but prints are much cheaper than bark. I'm not misusing my art at all, I hope I'm giving it more rather than taking away from it. Whenever I go to Canberra or wherever it seems like I'm a very busy person outside my community — but back at the community I'm just one of them. I'm not any better, I'm no more important than anyone else in the community. I'm just one of them, and I don't want to think that I'm better than my people.

I did start to receive criticism, not just from white art collectors but from some members of the community but I've always been true to my family. I've always looked at the copyright issues and I've always said if I am doing traditional art then I have to consult with my family. I have to consult with my family on the colours, how I'm representing the traditional art. Even though it's my own design based on my father's work, I still have to keep the traditional value in the art — and this means the colours, the people, the implements.

I suppose Aboriginal artists are coming out now more and more to talk about their art. Copyright is not because you're greedy and it's not because you want money, it's because the art represents the area you live in traditionally and because there's a boundary in the art which you can relate back to the land. There are certain guardians of the land and certain guardians of art; so you have to consult those people, you have to consult the traditional guardians of the land. There's also guardians for implements in ceremonial art, there's guardians for sacred things. That's why I'm not allowed to veer off from this art to a sacred family art. If I did then I'd have to have someone that looks over the art to make sure that I'm representing each colour and each line the correct way.

You've still got the old people who can't stand to see this happening; and then you've got a whole heap of contemporary people coming through, saying, "It's good, good that things are changing, a lot of things have changed, language changes, clothing changes." If there are changes to be made then it's okay as long as those changes are of quality, that's all I say.

There should be more of this new work going back to the local communities. More of it is exposed in European society and in the galleries than is going back to the community. If the works did go back to the community then maybe traditional people would understand a little bit more that it has to be contemporary art today, that we have to bypass old things to make new things so that in time it will get saved. My father's work has never been back home and it *needs* to be back home. I'm working on ways to do this. The National Gallery, of which I'm a council member, has offered to actually give it back for six months for an exhibition. My father was the first traditional man to come to one of the Sydney festivals in the early 1960s and give an exhibition of his work, but he's known best for his traditional role as a leader back home. He was always busy, he was the traditional clan leader of the community, controlling ceremonies, consulting different clan-groups about different things...

I'm working towards a stage now where I'm commissioning myself to do my own work and build up a collection and have an exhibition once or twice a year. I've only got one person I deal with in Sydney and I don't go to any gallery anywhere else because I don't find it necessary. Artists should be their own people, they shouldn't be controlled by other people. They should choose where they want to show. Traditional art is selling less because it's getting more expensive, but my work is the cheapest thing around. People want to buy it because it suits today's lifestyle, because they can take it home and frame it and hang it.

I am a council member at the National Gallery. The position opens a lot of doors. You can talk about almost anything concerning the running of the whole gallery. Council members are the ones who buy the works of art for the National Gallery, and there are at least twelve of us. It's the first time an Aboriginal has been in that position. I'm the only member in the gallery who is an artist and a council member. I hope that this appointment opens the way for other Aboriginal people to express themselves in other ways. I'd like to just share that achievement with the other Aboriginal people. I had a lot of help from other people, white and black, and I'm very thankful.

DOUG ABBOTT: *Artist*

Doug Abbott was born at Hermannsburg and is now based in Alice Springs. He combines working for the local council with painting with watercolours. A reformed alcoholic, he spends a lot of time lending support to people affected by alcoholism and counselling them. He is concerned by the lack of facilities made available for such a widespread problem.

I'm from Enbry station on the Finke River about 80 miles south of here. I'm forty-one, I was born at Hermannsburg, I speak Arunta and Western Arunta, I've done five years of schooling so I'm not that good at talking English. I'm getting used to it now, through getting around talking to people. I was ten-years-old when I started school, I didn't know a word of English when I started and then I picked it up from the other kids when I played with them. But I still can't pronounce some words properly.

When I grew up I got a job as a stockman. I left school when I was fifteen. My mum had some plans for me – I think they knew I was an intelligent young kid – but I said, "No, I want to be a stockman." I went out bush till I was about eighteen. Then I found out a bit more about town life, I messed around with the other boys, I got stuck into alcohol. I met my wife who I'm living with now, we went to Katherine and lived there. I worked on the railways, I was there for about thirteen months I think. I came back to Alice because my family was here and we got a commission home.

Then I went out bush, working with my family. I thought my wife and kids need a better future. Then I thought, station living isn't too safe: when you argue with the boss you're gone. So I thought I'd better go back into town, find a better job and a better house for my kids, for the future. That's when I got a job with the Town Council for a while – but then I stopped 'cause I was quite heavy into alcohol. So I found *another* job working out bush but I really missed my family; and then I found the dole.

The dole is the money that you can spend all day in the pub with. You just wait for the cheque to come, if you work for it you've got to work for eight hours a day. I thought it was a good thing, you know, that dole money. It was my big downfall I think.

In the end, when I was on the dole, I used to leave home early – before ten, and I'd go and find the boys ('cause I used to drink down the creek, in the laneways). That's when I started seeing my cousin, seeing him painting. I used to watch him paint. I've always been a good drawer. I used to see Albert Namatjira when I was a kid 'cause he used to invite my mum

**Centre and above: Painted dividers,
landscape, watercolour on board.**

over as soon as he sold a painting. He'd send a taxi over to pick us up and we'd have big watermelons and a big mob of tucker and we thought it was like Christmas, you know... I used to see him painting and when you're a kid you don't really take notice but that's where I picked it up from. I thought, seeing my cousin, I'm sure I can do that. So I did; I sold a couple of paintings, it just went on from there...

My body had had it after sixteen years of heavy drinking. About six years ago I said to myself that I wanted to stop but then I'd go out bush and when I come back I'd be straight back on the bottle again. I used to think, this is not good. I ended up in hospital a couple of times but it really didn't stop me; my *mind* was telling me I must stop but my *body* was crying out for that alcohol.

One day I went out bush — mum's got a little joint out by Hermannsburg — and I dried out for six weeks and had a good think to myself. I found out what was wrong with me...

Everything was wrong! I hadn't realised how seriously ill I was from alcohol 'cause I was on drugs at that time. I had alcohol poisoning, I couldn't move, I couldn't even walk, I had cramp in my back. So I came back to town. I was living in Charles Creek then, I was separated from my wife and my kids. And I really got on top of it.

The same time, I was painting. I spent more time painting, painting... I think that's what helped me. When you stop drinking you've got to have something to help you, or you go back drinking again. Whenever I got that silly idea of drinking I used to take up the paint brush and start painting the country. Now I just have to carry on. Old Albert started us all off; he painted this country like it was and I want to see this place stay the same, I don't want to see people cutting trees down, making roads and destroying our water holes forever. I want to see it as it is.

When I stopped drinking I went back to my wife and children. I locked myself in the house, I stayed in the house and watched telly all the time, not looking at what was going on outside. But I knew deep inside that people who drink need help. I know they need some place where they can go to — but we have no place for that in this town. I got a job as an alcoholic counsellor (when you stop drinking the job comes to you, you see) and then I ran into one of my white mates whom I used to drink with down the pub and we thought, why don't we have an Alcoholics Anonymous meeting. It might be a bit too late to save the older guys but surely we can help the younger generation with all our education programs on TV and video, with CAAMA (Central Australian Aboriginal Media Association) and so on. We have a lot of resources there that we can use.

I paint landscapes, my countryside, my country. I do Ayers Rock. In the old days if I'd done that I'd have been in big strife; but nowadays it's a popular thing for tourists. I put a big effort into my paintings, I don't rush anymore — when I was painting and drinking I used to rush for that time, you know... if I did a painting in the morning I'd be racing for ten o'clock before the bottle shop opened. But when you're not drinking you do a good job, you take your time, you put the work away if you feel a bit tired, then you come back and look at it again...

There is a lot of demand for well-known artists like Billy Stockman and others. They got a bit of a problem with alcohol and when you're drinking you do a quick job, just because your name's on it the people are buying it anyway, your work's going down hill, instead of improving. It's selling just because it's Billy Stockman or Clifford Possum, people are just buying it without looking at the quality of the painting.

We've got to make sure the paintings are good. Our watercolour artists, I think, are going to grow into something really strong with this dot or Dreamtime painting. But it's just too overdone you know; people in all walks of life are doing it, even the white people are doing it. Even white people with Aboriginal wives are doing it and putting their wife's name down... I don't want to say too much, but you've got to be very careful. The paintings are overstocked in this town, there's a lot of shops overstocked with the dot paintings — but with the watercolour painting, there's only a few artists and there's a bit more hope there...

When the Aboriginal watercolour artists formed a committee we had an exhibition in Fremantle. I saw my own work on the wall and the money came to me. When we used to do a painting and sell it to the shop-owners we never had anything back; but in Fremantle we met the buyers, saw our different styles, it was really good.

I just want the politicians to leave our land as it is and not to spoil it. We've got to start to wake up to ourselves, this earth is being destroyed worldwide and Australia is a real beautiful place here. I think it's about time we stop and think now. We're going too fast, we've got to slow down a bit. I do my paintings to show the world how beautiful this land is. There's that morning light, that midday colour, that really deep purple evening... It's time to stop, people are going too fast, building things, dams, houses, mowing down trees, damming water holes. I think we should learn to listen to old mother nature. I think we've got to start to wake up to ourselves. I think we should listen to the Aboriginal people. Forty thousand years we have lived here and we kept this country in one piece and we have never destroyed anything, you know. It's about time we stop — stop and think.

PANSY NAPANGATI: *Artist*

Pansy Napangati, originally from Haast Bluff now lives and paints in Alice Springs. She paints in the traditional dot style of the region, depicting the Dreaming stories of her mother and grandfather which were told to her by her uncle.

I was born at Haast Bluff and I came to Alice Springs about four years ago. I left because my people were fighting too much. I lost my family, they all died. I have no family, that's why I live here now.

It was once good at Haast Bluff, but not now. There are too many problems, like grog. It's bad because they drink, fight, have accidents when they are driving. It won't get better only worse. Papunya is a big place but no people are there now. Some artists have gone to Kintore, or some other place. There are a few in Papunya, like Michael Nelson.

I'm working in Alice Springs now. I help the people who want to understand how to vote. I explain the voting paper, how to fill it in and that kind of thing.

When I was a young girl, we always travelled around a lot – we'd go to a swimming hole, hunting, get bush tucker, tomatoes in a tree, beans in the ground, yellow, big and round. We'd get the seed and grind it with a stone, eat it or we'd cook it in the ashes. Mother was taken away a long time ago by another man, a half-caste man. My brother was a little baby. I was a big girl. I don't know where she went. I grew up with my sister, my nanna and my uncle. My dad was living with the Yuendumu side.

Mother's side was Lovtj people. After that I grew up and started learning for myself. Me and my friend always walked round to get bush tucker. We lived on the settlement mission. We rode the donkey, chased the nanny goats and drank their milk in the bush.

After that I grew up and started working. At Haast Bluff they taught me how to cook porridge and everything, and how to give it to the sick people. I did housework first and then after that I worked at the hospital. I got married but then I left my husband. I like to sit down by myself, there's too much trouble with a husband. I leave my little boy with his father. My son just came back now, a big boy, grown up. His father says, "You can have him now, I had little one, now you can have him." I was happy. He grew up in the bush, the old men looked after him – no school, nothing, but he's learning now, good school.

Later on I saw my uncle painting and I asked him, can you tell me my

Pansy Napangati (right) and her friend Pauline Nakamarra Woods, who was the first woman to be awarded the National Aboriginal Art Award.

Top: Pansy Napangati painting 'Two men' in her back garden in Alice Springs.
Above: 'Water snake story at Pikilli', acrylic on canvas.

mother's Dreamings. I want to put them down. He started to tell me how: "You can put them like that, this is your mother's, this is your Dreaming, two woman and one old man." I started, I was doing a painting. First I was painting but with glue and beans. After that I left glue and beans. I asked, "Where's my grandfather's country?" They tell me, "Your grandfather's Dreaming at the Hillbilly and your mother's one is Bush Mulberry." So I paint my grandfather's, and my mother's Dreaming, that's all I'm doing.

I put the paintings in the art gallery here, at Araluna. The first time he saw my paintings, this bloke, he buys my paintings. But they're taking all the paintings from here to overseas. White fella gets the money, we only get a little bit of money. White fella gets greedy, he should get half and Aboriginal people get half, but white people can't think like that.

I never learnt dancing and stuff. I always go to Church every Sunday. I'm thinking to start a story about what's happening now, about when my family was living and the mission was going out to the bush picking up the people, that's what I'm thinking.

MANDAWUY YUNUPINGUE:
Yothu Yindi Band

Mandawuy Yunupingue is the leader of the Yothu Yindi band. A powerful member of the Gumatj clan in Arnhem Land, he was the first Aboriginal man from the area to get a tertiary degree. He is now the principal of the community school at Yirrkala, 600 kms east of Darwin. Here he has implemented a new curriculum, combining traditional Yolngu (Aboriginal) teaching with the educational requirements of Balanda (white) society. His cross-cultural approach is being taken up in other parts of the Northern Territory.

Yothu Yindi, which means "mother and child" or "children of the earth", was formed in 1986. They were acclaimed at the 1988 South Pacific Arts Festival and at Darwin's inaugural Festival of Aboriginal Rock Music. They went on to play in North America and to represent Australia at the cultural olympics in South Korea in 1988. Their debut album is titled Homeland Movement.

Their performances include traditional songs and dances accompanied by an electrical rock sound, mixing drums and guitars with the Yidaki (didgeridoo).

I'm from the Yothu Yindi band, which comes from a place called Yirrkala in Arnhem Land. Sixteen languages are spoken there by sixteen clans. We come from a society that divides everything into two. The sixteen clans are divided into the Yirritja and the Dhuwa. I come from one of the eight clans in the Yirritja called Ganatj. We don't marry within our own clans, we only marry the opposite; the Dhuwa people. Basically Yothu Yindi means mother and child in both Dhuwa and Yirritja.

The time that I grew up was during the time that missionaries were colonising the place. People worked for flour and sugar in those days, but my father and mother still went out hunting for bush food. We used to go out in a canoe and walk great distances, always living off the land. Then education came and my mother used to encourage me to go to school so I could learn a bit of English and a bit of maths. The most important influence on my life comes from my traditional Aboriginal upbringing and it is this that makes me strong. I was brought up in the right way. Everything else doesn't really matter because I've got a strong foundation to start from. Everything I've got comes from there — my sense of identity,

Yothu Yindi performing in the United States in 1988 (photograph by Ned Lander).

sense of pride and the sense of integrity that connects me with my people.

Our development was encouraged by my own tribe. We are now good fighters, artists, and good politicians in a tribal sense. My father was a good singer, a good law maker; my brother is a big politician right now; and my sisters are right into bush medicine, they inform people of traditional herbs. I'm a teacher and a singer, it's part of my family background.

There are all sorts of things happening at a community level. We have our own social connections, tribal connections, relationships, extended relationships and languages that we're taught. We carry out circumcision, purification, cleansing, ceremonies as a part of our normal way of looking at things. Basically the community has adapted, as others have in other parts of the world, to being colonised and restricted by certain imposed rules and laws. Christianity played a big part in the colonisation process of our people, and what we're trying to do now is to decolonise ourselves.

Yothu Yindi has chosen rock 'n roll to sing about coming together and sustaining life so that it remains consistent with Mother Earth. Yothu Yindi is trying to bring about balance and in the process it tries to motivate people.

All my songs are focused on how we live — the times when white people took away our freedom. I want my music to give others an understanding of Aboriginal life and an idea of where we're coming from. Everything I write is derived from my traditional understanding. In setting up this band, my whole objective has been to try to combine together — the music of the past with the music of the future. Everything is centred on traditional music — the rhythm and the beat. We're trying to bring about an indigenous rhythm.

We might be able to offer something to the white community which I think is experiencing some kind of a dead end. We've got something to offer them. We've been patient and now it's our turn to offer something. Yothu Yindi is trying to do that through the language of music.

When you talk about the revolutionary things that have happened in the world, it's always been connected with art and I think the Aboriginal people are in that process now. Our art is a mechanism for change. What is it that we need? Change. Change in what? Change in attitude.

That is how we have to approach it. I think it's very important for us to connect with the land and mother earth, and I think it's important that we're strong in the area of music and art. I think if we can develop in those areas we can encourage others and bring about a better understanding, a more unified understanding.

TREVOR NICKOLLS: *Artist*

Trevor Nickolls began drawing as a young child, a habit encouraged by the psychiatrist his mother took him to see when he was eight-years-old.

After completing a Fine Arts Diploma at the South Australian School of Art, he trained further in South Australia and Canberra before becoming an art teacher. In 1980 he received a post-graduate diploma in painting from the Victorian College of The Arts, after which he took up a Creative Fellowship at the Australian National University.

His work looks visually at two central themes. One is the rapid development of technology and its damaging effect, relating this to the apparent balance, harmony and human dignity he sees as an integral part of the Dreamtime. The other is his own personal struggle in trying to reconcile his conflicting black and white heritage. In May 1990, Nickolls represented Australia at the Venice Biennale.

I was brought up at Findon on the way to Port Adelaide. My father was Irish and I've got Scottish, Spanish, Welsh and Aboriginal blood in me. When I was just a kid my mother's cookbooks were full of little drawings I did. At the age of eight my mother took me to a psychiatrist because she thought I wasn't seeing properly. He diagnosed St Vitus's Dance and used to give me scraps of paper to draw on. It was him who referred me to Saturday morning art classes. He realised I was using drawing to communicate. I discovered Picasso first — it wasn't until I was a teenager that I started studying Aboriginal art.

In my work I guess I'm trying to say how, just in our lifetime, white man and science and greed — greed for money — has made such a mess of this earth in terms of destroying nature... which is the most precious thing in Aboriginal society. My paintings are my Dreaming, my personal view of Dreaming. Looking at my paintings is like looking at my dreams.

I relate very strongly to trees and birds. In a lot of my paintings there's birds — because birds are the only thing we hear in this Machinetime. Aboriginal society is based on its relationship with nature, and the white man has made a mockery of that. The Dreamtime was a very structured society based on the laws of nature. Sure, there was good and bad — like there is in *every* society — but to me it seemed like a more balanced, respectful, dignified society than the one we have now. I haven't got any terms of reference other than what I've been brought up with in this lifetime in the suburbs... yet I feel that my spirit inside comes from

'Machine time nightmare', acrylic and oil on canvas.

another time, another space, that it's quite alien to this time. It's like I walk on a tightrope between the two, between what I know in this lifetime and what I know instinctively, inherently, in the other lifetime, the Dreamtime.

We live like robots. All isolated in our little cells, all in our little flats, tuned into the TV and technology, you come home from work, nine-to-five and push a button, TV: that's your connection. We're not educated to appreciate art, we're educated to act like robots, to use computers, to drive machines... and because of that we live such terrible spiritually defunct and culturally defunct lives and that's why I say Aboriginal art has such a value to give, why it's a gift to the world. We in Australia still have the Dreamtime spirit which pervades the psyche. People should be educated to appreciate the part that art and culture play in our life – it shouldn't be just for the rich, just for the elite, you know. In traditional society all you really had to take care of was your tucker; the rest of the time was spent in spiritual pursuits, creating art, discovering nature, meditating, evolving... Life should be a celebration, it should be about evolving within yourself.

My work is not purely Aboriginal art, it's a mixture. My work is cross-cultural and, as far as I'm concerned, by classifying it and saying it is Aboriginal art, by putting it in a box – well, that, to me, is racist. We have to break down that barrier. We have to evolve Aboriginal art as part of Australian art. I was brought up in a white society and went to a Western white art school, so my work is as much about Western traditions as it is about Aboriginal traditions. There has to be a breakdown of the barrier which insists on separating the two. Why can't my work be bought with the money from the contemporary Australian art budget? You tell me why. You tell me why, for the best bark paintings, you have to go to Germany. You tell me why the Pope has got a stash of Aboriginal paintings in his basement.

Pricing work is difficult, I hate it, I really hate it. Apparently my work has got a kind of market value, you know. *I* don't know, it's beyond me. I don't know how it's determined. I turn on the teletext on the TV to see how I'm going on the market, you know: "Oh Nickolls is down ten cents." "Oh," I say to myself, "What am I doing wrong, less dots, less dots, more cross hatching, that's it..." But I do feel like I'm reaching a point where I'm developing my own style. I've learnt from other artists: I've studied with Dinny Nolan, a Papunya artist; with Johnny Bulan Bulan, a traditional artist. I've looked at a lot of other people's work. Those Papunya paintings, those dot paintings – they're modern and yet they're ancient. I like cross hatching and dots. To make a dot is a very meditative thing. You come to feel the oneness of everything. The cross hatching is like working in space,

Above: Untitled. Right: 'Wrestling with white spirit', (one of a tryptich), oil and acrylic on canvas.

everything is broken up, floating, moving. They're appropriate in this day and age where you have all the electrical energy around and we can look at things in a molecular way. Modern dot paintings could have been done in New York yesterday, look how close they are to Pointillism and the use of the dot scientifically.

There has been a myth created by the anthropologists that traditional art was a static thing, but it wasn't — it was a continuing, evolving thing, the same as Western art. I don't use traditional symbols. They have big deep meanings and messages and they're pretty powerful forces you're mucking around with. I also think it's disrespectful. I explore as many avenues as I can with techniques but not with imagery. I believe that today you have to find your own symbols; the Machinetime we're living in today needs new symbols — and so you have to evolve, evolve... I use my own symbols, the buildings with the roofs that become jaws devouring the planet, a symbol I find becomes more prevalent as time goes by. I use four symbols regularly: the dollar sign, the crucifix, an antenna representing technology and a test tube for science. I think they are the four energies which are most at work in the world today. With the Dreamtime I use that head shape which I've used since I was a child. That serrated, sharp edge of a spirit being, screaming face upturned towards nature. Screaming, "What's happening? What have we done? What are we doing here?" It has references to Picasso's *Guernica* and Boyd's *The Bride Series.* It also deals with the fact that the white spirit is the dominant one in this age. Me being part black, part white, it's sort of like a wrestling I find I'm carrying on between myself in an attempt to keep my balance between the black and the white.

A picture has to tell a story. Art now is academic, it's intellectual, it's lost that power of communicating with us on our level, of telling us a story. It just does it for itself, for its own sake. I could never personally paint abstract; to me a picture is a story. Once upon a time, in traditional society, you'd go out into the bush before the corroboree, communing with nature, by yourself, getting ideas, then you'd come back and create a painting, then you'd present this painting at the corroboree. It's very hard being an artist in this society, you're on the fringe, you're a freak.

If there's to be a change in this society it has to come through art. Cultural revival means survival. We've wiped out all the beautiful knowledge we used to have. Now, suddenly, man is discovering he's lost all that knowledge. So now art has suddenly become precious to him. He's struggling to reconnect.

DELPHINE GEIA: *Centre For Aboriginal Studies in Music (CASM)*

CASM appeared first in 1969 in the form of a music centre established as a result of research by ethnomusicologist Cath Ellis. In 1972 this led to the formation of CASM, funded by the Aboriginal Arts Board, the South Australian Department for the Arts and the University of Adelaide. In 1975 CASM was integrated into the Faculty of Music at the University as a quasi-department. CASM has on average thirty to thirty-five students and the curriculum is based on a two-year Associate Diploma in Music. Many of the country's most well-known Aboriginal bands have come through or recorded at CASM. Most of the members of No Fixed Address, *for instance, were students of the Centre.*

An important part of CASM is its tribal teaching component. The Centre has close links with the Indulkana community in South Australia where a body of tribal people has accepted the responsibility for teaching non-Aboriginal students about Aboriginal music. Students and teachers from the Centre recently recorded a piece they named 'Urban Corroboree' mixing traditional and contemporary sounds and instruments. Whilst theory is an important part of the curriculum, much of the practical work is taught through traditional methods, listening and watching and imitating.

CASM was the precursor of various other Aboriginal music schools — AbMusic in Perth and the Broome Musicians' Association amongst others. Delphine Geia is a former student.

I see CASM as an Aboriginal music school for Aboriginal and Islander people from all over Australia, a school where they learn music and also have a chance to learn about Pitjanjatjara culture. It's a two-way learning process because people come from different parts of Australia. The Torres Straits Island culture is completely different to Aboriginal culture and you've got a whole cross-section of culture that meets at CASM. Torres Strait Island people, for instance, come down to teach their dances and their songs. The Torres Strait people themselves are divided up into three different parts and three different languages. And then of course we all learn Pitjanjatjara. Basically music is the common element.

What you learn depends on you as an individual. CASM is a place

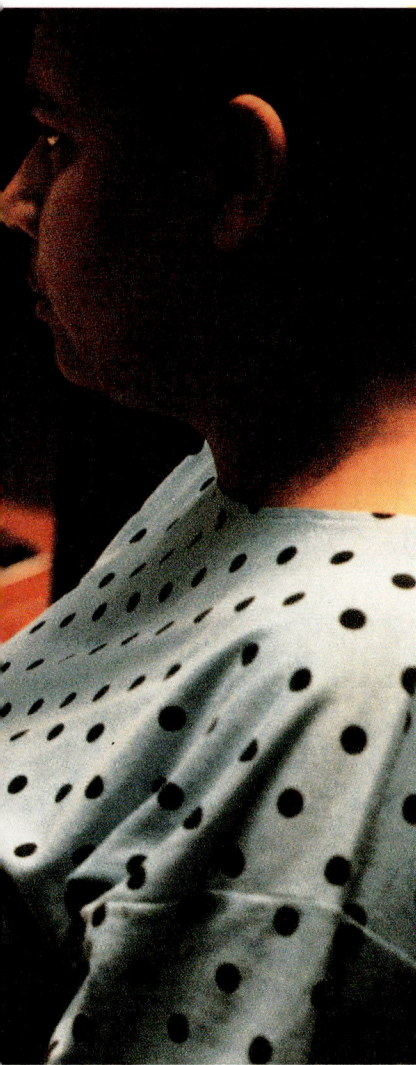

Left: Delphine Geia playing keyboards during the recording of 'Urban Corroboree'.
Below Left: Ladonna Hollingsworth, a student at CASM playing piano during the recording of 'Urban Corroboree'.
Below: Billy Mungie recording the tribal section of 'Urban Corroboree'.

where they not only teach the theory of Western music and its different styles but where they also encourage individual students to develop what *they* see as their musical talent. If you have an individual who prefers to use traditional music and build on that, or one who uses Western-style music but uses traditional language that's what's encouraged. There's not any general rule at CASM, it's whatever the individual wants to do.

To start off, the overall concept of 'Urban Corroboree' was to express how we felt about Aboriginal history — and that involved a composition of some sort in three phases. The first phase was the Dreamtime, that's where you've got the didgeridoo and then the flute with distorted sound coming in afterwards, using digital delay. Then you've got the other bit where civilisation happens and that's where you've got a sort of Western style — a fairly slow, laid-back piece, supposed to have an air of poignancy. After that there's the third part, which to me sounds like fast rock and a really bright sound. It's how the Aboriginal people want to deal with what's happened. And it's positive, it's getting on with life. It's too late to go back into the Dreamtime, so why bother with what might have been?

We go on a ten-day field trip to Indulkana every year and that involves us camping wherever the tribal elders allocate us to camp. The set up there is more one of order and authority, with the elders. It's almost like they have their own government. The elders had to get together and decide where we were to camp — but in my family the elders wouldn't be involved in that kind of process at all. They live a simple life. The things they worry about are things that are necessary to life, to survival.

We were quite lucky to have an *inma* put on for us in 1988. Everyone comes from miles around, it's a real honour to have one put on for you. It's a gathering together and dancing and singing. Depending on the different tribes and traditions, they have the women and men sing and dance separately.

The *inma* itself was great. The first one was magical, it was at dusk. We were staying about 20 kms out of Indulkana, just off the highway. And you could see all these cars coming from all directions. They had these big bushes on either side and they lit them up, it was just like a stage. Then someone would come out and put on the *inma*. They'd start dancing and singing and then they'd stop, then they'd turn their back to the audience and then they'd start again. The audience would be down one end, it's like an airstrip, all lit up and right from the other end the people with the body paints would come out: it looked like some kind of animal coming out. They had people with clapsticks up the front. We were told at the beginning to face the other direction and then to turn around – and there it was, all fires and dancers.

The women from CASM were asked by the Indulkana women there to join in and that meant taking our tops off and getting painted up. I was all set to do it, you know, but I'd misunderstood them. I thought we were just dancing for ourselves but we had to dance in front of *everyone* – and that meant everyone at CASM as well – and so I changed my mind and put my clothes back on. One of the older Indulkana ladies was quite insulted, almost to the point of anger. I couldn't explain that I didn't want to be topless in front of the guys that I go to college with. I *was* disappointed, but if it had just been in front of the women then that would have been alright, however we were behind the bushes getting painted up and the guys were already stretching their necks.

Things have changed a lot since the Bicentennial year. That was an advantage because it was like a world spotlight being shone on Australia and you had to look like you had your act together. Only time will tell if that will remain the same or if people will settle back into the comfortable role again – including the Government, I still believe a lot of white Australia would rather that there weren't any Aboriginals because then they wouldn't have to acknowledge that we were here first and that we're not as dumb as they would like to think. The majority of white Australians have to change a lot of their beliefs; it's not easy to do that.

It's an interesting time at the moment, I've got a brother who's an artist and Aboriginal art is in great demand now. Every man and his dog is going out to buy Aboriginal art, and it's trendy to like Aboriginal people. A lot of people are saying, "I've got an Aboriginal friend," just like they'd say "I own a black Porsche."

But the abuse comes from both sides obviously: I've known some Aboriginal people to paint a house and just because they are Aboriginal they call it Aboriginal art! Aboriginal art should be taken seriously – and if people are serious about lifting the quality of life for Aboriginal people, then that sort of thing should be controlled, and we should encourage the change since 1988 to be not just a flash in the pan.

If we don't take proper advantage of what's happening and we just abuse it then we'll have to try twice as hard to function in mainstream Australia in the future. There's such diversity amongst Aboriginal people it's hard to get a collective agreement of all Australian Aboriginals. That, coupled with white Australia's general attitude, is going to make it terribly hard for us after all this trendiness dies down...

EASTERN AUSTRALIA

'The lamppost', Karen Casey.

STEPHEN PAGE: *Dance Teacher and Choreographer*

Stephen Page was a student at the Aboriginal Islander Dance Theatre who subsequently became one of its teachers. Whilst he was a student most of the teachers were European; he sees his own teaching role as part of those important changes that are taking place in the structure of the dance company. Stephen has choreographed various public performances. He also works periodically with the Sydney Dance Company and has appeared in their production Soft Bruising *in April 1990. He has plans for travelling with a group of dancers to Aboriginal communities: he hopes to produce a new show based on a cross-cultural exchange between tribal and urban Aboriginal dancers. Stephen currently lives and works in Sydney, New South Wales.*

My father is from the Mullinnjarli tribe; he came from a small place called Beaudesert which is in the southern part of Queensland. My mother is Maori and Aboriginal and she's got a bit of English and Spanish blood as well. They had twelve wonderful children — six girls and six boys — and I was the third youngest. My father didn't teach us much about the culture, he was just surviving, he was a builder's labourer — and just looking after twelve children was enough for him. The funny thing is that though we struggled in our family, entertainment was always a big thing, you know. Mum and dad always would tell us stories. We couldn't afford to go to the pictures and things like that, so my sisters used to put shows on for us. There was always that kind of theatre in our family, we all used to sing and dance. My father used to do a bit of traditional dancing. We had a good upbringing: with a big family you're really close and communication is a really important thing. We were always told to communicate, no matter what happened to us.

It was the Dance Company which brought me to Sydney. I saw one of its posters, at the time I didn't even know there was a black dance company — that's when things were just getting set up in black theatre. Sydney was the place, I told myself. So I auditioned and got in and did three years.

The dance theatre has a raw and unique style — you don't really rely on technique, it's the focus and the feeling that come out, it's *all* internal. You never see a traditional dancer warming up before he does traditional dance; he's just up and it's there. It's such a strong spiritual thing, it's so old in a way — I always feel old when I do traditional dance. It's what comes behind it, I think, it's the environment, the sounds, the didgeridoo, the songman... it's all that preparation that makes it work.

I have a project I'm working on. I want to take six urban dancers to traditional areas and try to create a whole work from that. Traditional tutors come down to the school sometimes. It's a shame that we keep performing in an indoor theatre. I'd love to have an outdoor theatre. An outdoor theatre is like bringing back old theatre; of course I don't know what old theatre was really like — but in a sense it was always an outdoor performance. I think that's the only way you can capture the essence of our contemporary style... it's by seeing it performed outdoors, in natural lighting. I'd love to use the full moon as a light.

So I want to take a designer and a lighting guy with me to all these communities so we can create this work. What I want to do is get a lighting designer and a set designer so that the work has a contemporary feel with a traditional flavour. The lighting man here, Mark Howard, is Aboriginal. He's the first one who's lit traditional dance in indoor theatres — and to do this he's sat with traditional people and talked to them, about what time of day it's supposed to be and the environment and all the natural things... It's the same with set design: I was speaking to Raymond Meeks who's an urban artist and set designer and *he's* interested in building ant hills.

A lot of urban blacks are frightened of using traditional dance. There's been discussions and cultural meetings where they're worried about the contemporary world taking over the traditional and using traditional material in a bad way. What I'm saying now is, we have to have an urban style, an urban identity as well. We can't do traditional dance unless we go and take it from the North — but then there's friction there, you know, because all you're doing is taking, taking the northern people's dance. I went to Yirrkala and they said, where's your traditional dances from down there? And I had to explain to them that it's all gone. Mind you, now what's happening in Yirrkala is that the young ones up there are generating new traditional dances: when they first saw a flag they started doing a flag dance; and when they learnt how to play cards they did a card dance. So it's like the next generation of traditional dancers developing these new dances and this in fact is the same thing that *I* want to do. My choreography is basically fantasy, it's all dreams; and that's what basically we're all about...

The style which I'm teaching to my students now in class is of animals — very contemporary movement. A lot of the movement I teach is into the ground, into the earth movement. Another thing I'm looking at is

**Stephen Page rehearsing for a production with the
Sydney Dance Company.**

traditional bodies: they are completely different to the anatomy that we're all so used to. The Aboriginals can keep their heel on the ground for so long without even lifting it off while they squat on the ground... it's amazing to watch. When I first joined the company that was something that hit me and I started working on it. I worked out a little routine on how we could develop it, I started looking at students' legs. I thought, they've all got it. What we have to do is find the movements that can fit our bodies. Another thing we've done is to spend a whole day in a parallel line and concentrate. That was one of my queries about traditional dance. How they just focus, stare for so long, and then that focus is gone somewhere else... That's the style I want to develop, the feeling of that focus. I'd really love to develop this technique, perhaps in ten or twenty years' time I can open it to the public so it's not just an urban Koorie technique. I think in Australia, especially in dance, people are looking for that. The Sydney Dance Company base themselves on classical techniques, yet their choreography has a strong contemporary feel. The essence derived from traditional dance fused with contemporary movement is probably what's needed as this country's own technique, rather than relying on the influence of European and American dance styles.

Theatre-wise, things are just beginning. When you go and see black theatre today it's always the same issue of looking for land rights and at the white onslaught and looking at our ancestors and our mothers all being raped... But we can't dwell in the past anymore, we have to create stories now where it's positive, where blacks aren't the blacks that you see in gutters, where blacks are now *controlling* things. There's a younger generation of Aboriginals who are all getting their HSC and who want to be doctors and lawyers. I think that's important, I think in the arts what we have to do is portray those things too — through social-comment theatre.

For our end of year show we did something called "Television Stories" which is about the influence television has on the urban society. When I was in Maninngrida they had the television sets out in the sand and everyone just sat out there and watched it and I thought "God, it's such an addiction". So we did a piece on it: it was a new item, dealing with a different subject but it had a positive end. That's the kind of social-comment theatre that I'm looking for. I mean, come on now it's the 1990s!

I think we have to show our skill in theatre. We can't just get away now with stories of murder and depression, people just think that's a weak way out really — showing the negative side of life. We can't wait for time anymore, we really have to move, we have to get our creativity out — and not just in Australia but internationally too.

EUPHEMIA BOSTOCK: *Artist*

Born on the far north coast of New South Wales at Tweed Heads, Euphemia Bostock, known as Phemie to her friends, is one of five children. Her brothers, Gerry and Lester Bostock, are both well-known. Her mother is from the Bunjulung people of the Grafton–Lismore area and her father from the Munanjali people near Beaudesert, south-west of Brisbane.

In 1962 Phemie came to live in Sydney as a single parent with her two children and worked in a handbag factory. During the 1960s and early 1970s she was involved in the Aboriginal struggle which saw the early formation of the now established Aboriginal Services. During that time she became interested in theatre and in the arts.

Phemie has worked in sculpture, linoprints and screen printing on paper and fabric for many years, incorporating textured surfaces, ink wash and printing. Today she is concentrating on her fabric design, which are often large pieces of coloured tie-dyed silk. She is a founder of Boomalli Aboriginal Arts Co-operative.

I was born in Tweed Heads; my growing-up time was a wonderfully happy time. My father was a main roads construction worker so my mum would pack everything up and we'd move in tents wherever dad worked on the roads. We did a lot of that in my very early years. When I was about eight or nine, I suppose, we went to live in Brisbane. I didn't have much of an education because in those days Aboriginals weren't expected to stay at school. As soon as I turned thirteen I left school and went into factory work, then I got married. Husband left me, I had a child, had two children.

In Brisbane in the 1960s the credit squeeze was on and it was hard to find work. I was living on a deserted wife's pension, which was nothing. I read in the paper that there was a lot of work in Sydney so I came down, landed here in the morning, walked into a handbag factory by 11 o'clock.

In those days it was cardboard boxes and fruit crates we'd sit on. I remember the first Christmas in Sydney, I had nothing to give the kids and I just painted the boxes. Gee, I'm still getting emotional about this. Those days were hard but I had a lot of good friends who saw me through. I even had a wonderful friend who was a prostitute and I didn't know about it. She used to arrive on my door and say, here's the clothes and the food for the kids. Mum and dad arrived shortly after that and things started getting better...

In those days, in the Glebe area, there was a lot of interaction between artists — black artists, just starting up. All this time that I've been involved

Above: Euphemia Bostock at the home of Bronwyn Bancroft in Sydney.
Right: Euphemia Bostock with one of her hand printed pieces of silk.

with the Aboriginal community I've seen a lot of changes since I came in 1962. And I can tell you, we had nothing then. We used to walk around and do doorknock appeals and raise money by having barbecues in people's backyards. Then we'd go to the government and say, "Give us a dollar for every dollar we raised." We had a lot of conferences.

I was the tea-lady, never the person who stood up to talk! Since then I've been developing — doing little things, weaving, leisure-time classes, sculpting... Sculpture is my love. I don't know how I get my shapes, I just sit down with a knife and start carving and if something comes out then I go with it. I've got these figure-images, like a woman giving birth. I guess that comes from when my dad used to tell me stories about how creation came — about the three sisters who gave birth to the tribes.

A lot of the active people from the 1970s have ended up in the arts: acting, writing poetry, writing, making films, painting. I think the arts has given us a purpose. I have often felt that I've got to be justifying myself and I don't want to be doing that. I think it's got a lot to do with an education system that teaches us that "real" Aboriginals are tribal Aboriginals living up north. They say we've got no culture — but we have an urban culture that's a combination of what our fathers and mothers have taught us and our lives here now. We've still got our keepers that have kept legends and stories and passed them on. And we've still got a lot of real old people throughout NSW who are still telling the old stories, passing them on down. It's a different level of culture but it's just as truly Aboriginal.

I think, though, we need to have a national conference with the traditional artists. When you're going through art school you have your masters. Now, *they* are my masters. We should pull visual and performing artists from all over Australia and get them down here, we should have the traditional artists say "these are the ground rules" cause we down the South have never been given any direction on how to go. The young ones that are coming up, they see a traditional image and they use it without realising what is social and what is religious. I think we all have to be given guidelines to work with and I think you have to have a national assembly of visual and performing artists to do that.

I reckon the Government could to it. The way they get tourists here is purely through the Aboriginals, through their painting, through the Northern Territory, through Kakadu... It is Aboriginal culture that brings most of the tourists to Australia; so just on that alone it would be just pocket money for the Government to pull all the artists together.

We're pulling together at Boomalli. The wonderful thing about Boomalli is that everybody there teaches each other, sharing ideas and techniques. To me, it *is* an art school. I'm just glad to be part of the group, there's a real companionship between us. I was introduced at a gallery opening a few weeks ago and they said I was the elder of the tribe! I laughed at the time but I've been thinking about it since and I feel really great that they said that. We *are* a little tribe there and we share, we exchange information with each other. It's becoming an educational place: schools come to us, international visitors are starting to come and get educated.

It's a little bit different from walking into an upmarket gallery, looking at the paintings and walking out again. We *are* a gallery, but I think we want to be more of a community education base as well. Boomalli is driving to link an all Aboriginal network. The beautiful thing that's happening about Boomalli is that the ordinary urban Aboriginals are coming in to purchase pieces of work. They might take six months to pay it off but they're buying it. To me that's the thing, they're now starting to appreciate their own urban art. Even the street kids, they just come in and have a quick look. Over the next few years I want to see Boomalli strengthen and grow more independent.

Personally, I want to develop my sculpture. In 1991 I would like to have a solo show, basically sculpture. I don't think that's really been touched on in urban Koorie art. I'd like to work in bronze. My major aim is to pay tribute to our people — to our returned servicemen who were not citizens of this country but who went to war, who fought for this country and were never acknowledged. They've got monuments here for the Japanese people yet they haven't got one for the Aboriginals and the Torres Strait Island men who went and fought for this country.

I'd like to make monuments to the road construction men, the railway men, the cane-cutters, the stockmen. I don't know how I'm going to do these things but our fathers and our fathers' fathers built this nation doing railway work, doing construction work, in the cane fields, all these sorts of things... So somewhere along the way I'd just like to see tribute being paid to them, that's my aim.

Note: This interview was conducted with Bronwyn Bancroft at her shop Designer Aboriginals in Balmain.

LIN ONUS: *Artist*

Lin Onus left school at thirteen and worked with his father for several years in arts and crafts, which they sold through his father's shop in the Dandenongs in Victoria. During this time he had a lot of contact with visiting artists and craftsmen. Lin later worked as a motor mechanic, panel beater and spray painter before experimenting with oil paints that he had found at his home. Sherbrooke Forest provided his early visual stimulus.

Lin had his first show in 1975 at the Aboriginal Advancement League in Melbourne and has since exhibited regularly. Currently he is chairman of the Aboriginal Arts Board and very involved with newly emerging bureaucratic structures which deal with new issues such as copyright, funding and curatorial control. Lin currently lives and works from his studio/home in Upwey, Melbourne, Victoria.

I was born in Melbourne but lived extensively in other parts of Australia. My father used to have a shop near here making artifacts and souvenirs and we'd always had artists working for us. I suppose I watched them and without realising it at the time I was probably learning for later. Like most children I didn't want to work with my dad so I became a motor mechanic. When my dad died I tried to carry on the business, I'm not a businessman, so that didn't work. It was sometime later that I started painting. I found some student oil paints at home and did a painting of Sherbrooke forest which I sold at the Arts Society, things went on from that beginning really.

I often look back at my re-emergence as an artist. I was a landscape artist until 1986 and I happened to find myself in Maningrida and met Jack Wunuwun, who has since become my father. Jack was very concerned that people down in the South had lost their law, language and culture. He felt rightfully that there must be some sort of void there and he wanted to help fill it. In relation to this Jack was most anxious to educate me and that was the start of our three-year-long relationship. I've been back to Maningrida twelve times since and Jack has taken on a mentor role.

You go through an initial naming process when you first become involved in the community and after two or three years you might go through a second naming process which is what happened to me. This is a very specific and personalised name and it bonds you to a particular family group. The whole experience has had considerable impact on me and I think it's reflected in my work and in my attitude to life which has changed considerably since. I tend to be much more laid back about things and have

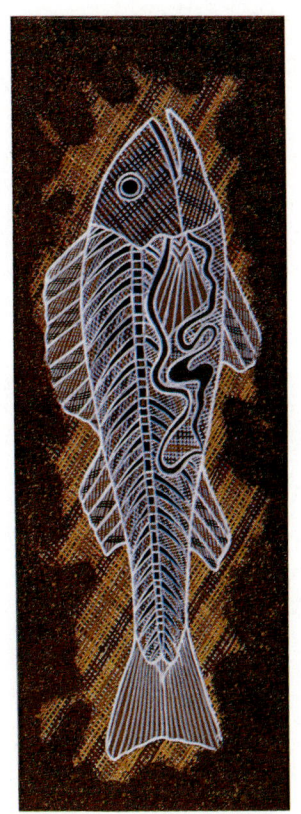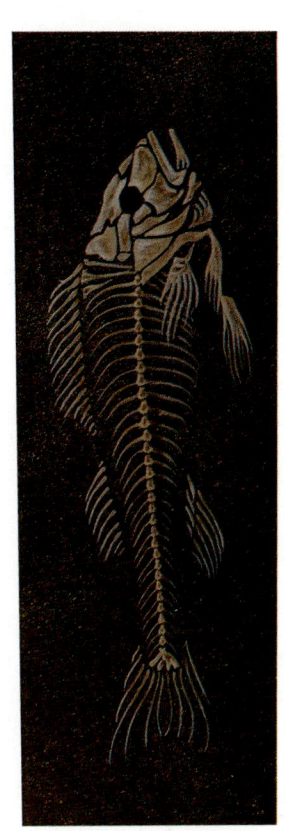

'Fish' (Tryptich), 1988.

Top: 'Night sky at Gamerdi', 1988, Art Gallery of Northern Territory.

a much deeper sense of belonging to a place, something people in Sydney and a lot of people in Victoria feel a deep lack of. In many instances their grandparents had moved around the country to avoid the native police who were taking the children away at that time. My relationship with the country is now at a place called Gamerdi outstation in Central Arnhem Land and it's like a missing piece has clicked into position and I like that.

The traditional stimulus from this experience is apparent in my work in the use of cross hatching from Central Arnhem Land and the way I mix realist imagery with traditional imagery from the top end. Each time I go to Gamerdi it's like I've served a bit more apprenticeship and I can then paint more things and the longer the relationship goes on the more access I have to imagery. I also inherit imagery from John Bulun Bulun who's my other father. I think that traditional art will remain the foundation on which everything is built but we all draw from a variety of influences. Trevor Nickolls also had a great influence on me, he was right out there in the vanguard, long before it was even fashionable. It must have been pretty hard for him in the early days.

A visit to Japan had a lot to do with the fish imagery I use. I taught there for ten days with Ellen Jose and I'd always been fascinated by the paradoxes in Japanese society. During the war years they saw themselves as very aggressive but would, at the same time, perform a tea ceremony that might last for hours. I found myself watching their television at different times of the day. Japanese children would watch an awful lot of horror movies, the sort of stuff we wouldn't allow during children's viewing times in Australia. Yet Japanese children don't seem to be particularly affected by that. These paradoxes were interesting particularly in relation to their environment which is full of smog, chromium and glass and yet people are really into tending gardens; they have gardens the size of a dinner plate. A garden isn't complete without a pond and much less complete without a fish. I did a fish painting whilst I was there and the fish images keep coming back to me in various ways. The next phase was to paint the fish to make them traditional in some sort of way, because if I didn't do that I'd just be painting a fish. So that was really the start of the fish paintings.

I've started to work more frequently in three dimensional mediums. I'm actually getting a bit sick of painting, or perhaps dissatisfied is a better way of putting it. You can't interact with a painting like you can with something that has three dimensions. There's a sculptor in me that wants to get out.

As far as the increasing interest in Aboriginal art in general goes, I think two things happened simultaneously. Firstly, there's the growing realisation of Aboriginal people themselves that art is a viable career option. Up until about ten years ago, if you talked about careers for Koories it was along the line of "You too can be a garbage collector" or "We can teach you how to clean white people's houses." Somewhere along the line people said, "No, we don't have to do this," and started to go off in different directions. Now there's quite a number of Aboriginal people going off to law school, to medical school. I also think that at about the same time when our people thought about making a commitment to their art rather than the factory floor. At that same time a very small group of white Australians — and it's *still* a relatively small group — became prepared to vote with their hip pockets. So it required two things happening: the artist to produce; and the people to support the artists.

I have mixed feelings about the sudden popularisation of Aboriginal art. As an artist I'm pleased to see that my peers are surviving as artists. On the other side, wearing my hat as chairman of the Aboriginal Arts Committee, there is some concern that current practices in remote areas do not necessarily serve the long term needs of developing artistic movements. In some remote areas the new generation of art dealers includes former mechanics, policemen, real estate agents, station owners, government administrators and so on. The Committee is worried that the presence of a multitude of dealers could ultimately weaken, rather than strengthen, the developing process. The Arts Committee is also concerned with issues like copyright. We want to have a strong international profile. Many people are taking Aboriginal art overseas, not all but some of them are the same old bad guys who were showing the mediocre work in Australia and asking high prices for it. I think the market in Australia is becoming more discerning and they're just moving off shore. I think it's up to us to chase after them and try and tidy it up in some way and present a better aspect overseas.

I think the sort of thing that I would like to see, first and foremost, is the development of Koorie entrepreneurs, at least a level of Aboriginal curatorial control. The direction of Aboriginal art is still being determined by non-Aboriginal experts. There's really only the one Aboriginal curator in Australia — John Mundine at Ramingining. If we're really going to have any sort of degree of self-determination then we have to develop a level of expertise and try and get people into those positions so that they can be arbiters of fashion or decision-makers. The paradox is that most Koories interested in the arts would rather be involved as a producer rather than as middleperson or salesperson. So that's a dilemma as well, but at least entrepreneurship is starting to appear.

BRONWYN BANCROFT:
Artist and Designer

Bronwyn Bancroft grew up northern New South Wales and completed her Higher School Certificate in 1975. In 1980 she finished a Diploma in Visual Arts at the Canberra College of the Arts.

Bronwyn is known best for her fabric prints, which she sells through her own company and shop, Designer Aboriginals. Her business is not only successful but fulfils other personal aspirations: it provides an opportunity to employ and encourage younger artists and places the control of the marketing of Aboriginal products back into Aboriginal hands.

Bronwyn is a committed member of the Boomalli Aboriginal Artists Co-operative and has recently moved from prints to painting. Her work is vibrant and very much a reflection of her personality. She currently lives in Balmain, Sydney.

Ever since I was a kid I've believed I was going to do art. At art school I did this turtle design with all these skyscrapers and then all these Aboriginal faces pushed in the concrete. This woman teacher came up (she was a fairly formative painter at that time) and just put a big stroke through it and said, "That's shit, you're not allowed to do that at this art school." So what they did was they oppressed my Aboriginality, they told me I wasn't a proper Aboriginal. I had a good tan but I wasn't a proper Aboriginal! I rang my husband and he convinced me to go back. I did go back — and I did exactly what they wanted me to do. Then after two years I developed my own way of photography which was really textural, it was made up of all these tiny little figures that were all photographed and then reduced so you'd have about a million figures in one picture...

In terms of my work I think I've done what essentially every artist has to do: that is, I've developed a language, a language that then becomes identifiably your own symbol-making. I've developed a large variety of symbols and a fluency in my work. I think that to take images belonging to other groups and just copy them brings no development for the artist. I know that I'm not compromising myself in what I believe about traditional art; in fact I'm *elevating* traditional art by making a statement that is contemporary and that is personal.

Urban artists tend to believe that the traditional people are the leaders with their work, because their work is so pure. However, I think a lot more

Top: 'My molecular madness', gouache on rag paper.
Above: Bronwyn Bancroft and Danielle Gorogo silk-screening T-shirts at Bronwyn's shop Designer Aboriginals.

135

urban people now feel far more assertive about their rights as artists, they have gained a lot more self-esteem. We're asking art circles not to accept us as just Aboriginal artists, we're asking to be accepted as *professional* artists. We really believe that we've got something to offer people on a professional level, we don't want to get by on an Aboriginal ticket.

In terms of the future directions for Aboriginal art, there are probably several levels of concern. Aboriginal people have to develop a rapport between traditional artists and urban artists, they have to create a platform where they come together and discuss what's happening in the arts industry, and they have to do this without intervention from non-Aboriginals. Take the urban artists: some of them don't understand traditional imagery, so we've got to get them together with traditional people. That way you develop a nationwide respect and an arts industry that's going to help Aboriginal people throughout the country. I think there will be another flurry of popularity for a while and then in 1991 it will die down. The general public will become more discerning; and that's when artists are going to have to pull up a little bit and produce really good work, because by that stage there may be another twenty new young artists!

The whole field is virtually untapped. I don't think the Australian Government or the Australian arts industry or the Australian Art Gallery or the general population have any idea about what Aboriginal people are capable of. We've been repressed for so long. We've got to make sure our work is put into the places where it *should* be put — into good galleries, into other places where people can see it like the new Parliament House. The curators should buy a mixture of urban art and traditional art. Contemporary art needs to be in a public viewing place. We need to move away from this romantic idea that only tribal work is of value. Give the urban people fair money for fair work; you don't have to give them welfare, you don't have to give them anything; just give them something for their art.

I think Boomalli (Aboriginal Artists Co-operative) has got an incredible potential and I don't think we realise it ourselves. We're going to be developing things not only for NSW but for Australia and internationally. The place will become internationally known because we've got the guts to stand up and say, "We're going to have a go, don't knock us." We're not the Julian Ashton art school but we are trying to develop a formative base for all Aboriginal artists. We can access a lot of material and we can affect a lot of public opinion so we *will* get there if we learn how.

Administration is our only flaw but I think we've learned a lot this year.

One critical point is that Aboriginal artists have got to help other Aboriginal artists. As individuals we will only be successful for a short time. But, if you put in your bid with your contemporaries who are working with you then you can develop something that will go on for our children and *their* children. My belief is that whatever you do — whether it's internationally acclaimed or not — you don't aspire to do that for your own good, you do it so that when you've gone up the ladder it makes it a little bit easier for someone who is coming behind you. Whatever an Aboriginal person does to break into an area is a great and good thing and I applaud, but that person should remember that they're only opening the door for somebody else. I think Aboriginal people are changing and they're really trying to support each other. Now that's something that's really important to a culture that's been diminished like Aboriginal culture has been.

BRIAN SYRON:
Film and Theatre Director

Brian Syron initiated the first Australian National Playwright's Conference on the ABC series Seven Little Australians, *where he was acting coach and casting adviser. He was awarded a scholarship to study in Poland with Gersi Grotowski and later he trained as a director of film on TV with the BBC in London. He also worked with Cecily Berry (voice teacher to the Royal Shakespeare Company). Originally he was trained by Stella Adler in New York during the 1960s.*

Brian has been consultant to the Aboriginal Arts Board of the Australia Council since 1972. He helped open the Black Theatre in Redfern and founded the first National Black Playwrights conference and also the Aboriginal National Theatre Trust. Brian received the Harold Blair award for a lifetime achievement in the performing arts.

In 1989 he was awarded the Ikimman *(Sacred Eagle Feather Symbol) for the quality of his contribution as a participant in "The World of Aboriginal Motion Pictures" in Canada. He is currently living in Sydney and directing a new feature film,* Jindalee Lady.

I'm from Minimbah which is seven miles up the river from Foster, which is 200 kilometres north of Sydney. I grew up alternating between Balmain, where I was born, and Foster — with my Aboriginal grandmother. I was also exposed to the missions at Purfleet and Foster and travelled with my grandmother visiting uncles and aunts. She was full-blood; she taught me many things about the old ways and traditions and so did her brothers and sisters. So I was very, very fortunate.

I remember when I was a small child, one day we'd gone to Foster to get supplies. (The old lady knew about what would happen to me, and she wasn't wrong. I was in three institutions and a maximum security prison before I was seventeen.) Anyway, we were going along in the boat and we got home and she said, "You bring in those supplies," then she walked to the top of the hill under the fig tree and said, "Okay, put the bags down." I put the bags down, bread and flour and things like that. She said, "You come here boy" and then she added, "You see this tree?" I said, "Yes." "This tree is taree, it means sacred fig tree in the old language." And I said, "Yes." She said, "Now you put your arms around this tree like me," and she put her arms around the tree and I put my arms around it. I was smaller than her, I was about seven. She said, "You look at me now," and I said, "Yes." And I looked into her face and she said, "When I die my spirit's going to come here and live in this tree." She continued: "When you have trouble in this lifetime with the white man, and you're going to have trouble because you're a cheeky boy, you just come here you put your arms around this tree and you talk to me, I'm here."

You don't come back from that, you don't come back from an experience like that. The anger I had, later in life, it was healthy. But I have no mortgage on suffering, I have no mortgage on being dispossessed or having had a tough life. We've *all* had it. Every Aboriginal person I know of in my generation has had one hell of a time. Nobody has a mortgage on that. We've all been through it. A very wise woman told me once: "Bitterness is like rust, like old rust, it will rot your body away." You can't hang on to that kind of bitterness, you gotta have hope.

I started the first playwright's conference and two years later when we had the second one you should have seen the work that came through. It was wonderful: there was stuff by Colin Johnson and Richard Walley and Jimmy Chi, it just came in waves — wonderful work, really good work. Themes for Aboriginal playwrights are limitless. The anger will always be there, it will always be there, I mean, that's always part of the dispossessed — but now we have to examine ourselves as people. I'd like someone to put on the stage a play that involves Charlie Perkins and what he's been up to and Pat O'Shane and what she's been up to and government ministers and previous ministers so we can really start to see, at the grass-roots level, how that begins to affect people. We can't blame the whites too much more, we've got an emerging black bureaucracy that is every bit as bad and — to me — least forgivable of all because they should know better and unfortunately a lot of times they don't. That I think is the saddest thing of all, the mistakes that your own people perpetuate and please quote me on that. That's the danger. The arts should be used to focus on what's going on in Aboriginal society, not just apportioning blame. As Shakespeare says in Hamlet's speech to the players: the purpose of playing is, as it were, to hold the very mirror up to nature, to show virtue her charm and so forth and so on, you know. I think we've not only got to do that, we've also got to examine what we're doing in terms of what we're playing for. I mean do we mount productions to be acceptable at the Belvoir Theatre, the Victorian Arts Centre, the Adelaide Festival? Who cares? What is our obligation, what is our mandate? It's back there in the resolutions of the Aboriginal Arts Board in 1972: our mandate is to communicate with our own people first.

Top: Brian Syron at work on the set of *Jindalee Lady*.

You don't elevate a people by pandering to the middle class.

I think the best thing that has happened in black theatre is the emergence of well-trained and professional actors. I mean the fact that Ernie Dingo has become a sex symbol, I think that's very healthy, he's very talented and very good. But I don't think near enough is good enough, I cannot accept an inadequate performance and say, that's our way. It's *not* our way, not at all. I think that's a cop-out, coming from the blacks. You have to have discipline, you have to have a technique, you have to move forward, you have to understand that you are mirroring a society and that what you are playing is not just a WA or a northern NSW or an Alice Springs black. What you are playing is a symbol of Aboriginal men and women in this country, the condition of our people. That's something bigger than us and I think sometimes our ego can get in the way. I think that that has to be learnt by our people — and fortunately it *is* being learnt. Now you've got a lot of disciplined people coming out of the dance theatre, you've got a lot of actors coming through institutions where they understand the nature of theatre and they're very disciplined.

I think the development of the arts does put the reviewer or critic in a very bad position because often they don't know anything about the Aboriginal world. They haven't got a clue because they haven't been told about it, they've learnt nothing in history. The arts are embryonic and yet people still don't know the conditions from which they have grown and so it makes criticism very difficult. When the critics see an inadequate production or inadequate acting, what standards are they supposed to judge from?

Film is the most lasting thing. Every major film director in this country has done their black film, their film on Aboriginals. And they've failed. They've failed because of two things; they've underestimated the intelligence of the men, and they've depicted the women totally without any dignity. I think the only one of the major directors who hasn't done a film about Aboriginals is Gillian Armstrong — and I think that's because she's smart enough as a woman to know she doesn't know enough about the Aboriginal world. *Fringedwellers* by Bruce Beresford, *Eliza Fraser* by Tim Burstill, *The Last Wave* by Peter Weir... they're all middle-class. There's no working class in this country, no real working class. There are no major social problems, so they come in on the black area, where there are major social problems and so they're interpreting a lower working-class world from a middle-class mentality. They've got to fail because they don't know it. It's the same as if you take someone who's coming out of the British aristocracy or some rich guy who has grown up in Virginia and goes to do his film on the Holocaust. How the hell can he understand what it means to be a Jew in Nazi Germany.

I have no doubt the interest of white people in Aboriginal art will be sustained because they know they have no art, they know they have no culture, they know they have no tradition. Regardless of the pretence they put up there, they don't have it. They can't walk out of a house and see a building that's five-hundred years old. They know that if this country has a spirit it's Aboriginal. If there is any tradition of art here it is Aboriginal. This country is barely two-hundred years old and this generation of young people are the first who have suddenly been made aware of what the white man's policy was here and what they did to our people. This generation of Australians are aware of the fact that they have been robbed, that they have been lied to by their system of education, that it has not told the truth of how this country was settled and what happened to the indigenous people. I think this young generation of creative artists will contribute much, much more. I think they will have more to contribute and they don't have the same problems to face — we've done it for them, we've broken through, the Marcia Langtons, the Bobbi Sykes, the Gary Foleys, the Dennis Walkers have broken down the doors and they're walking through and that's great.

I think what's happening *is* great, I can see the discipline coming out of places like the Aboriginal Islander Dance Theatre, I think there's a real sense of professionalism. I think the discipline is coming. I think that's what we've got to get together is professionalism. And if we do, then we can make the work sing from the stage and we can move forward to what Mr Jimmy Chi calls a *Bran Nue Dae* . . .

KAREN CASEY: *Artist*

Karen was born in 1956 in Hobart, Tasmania. She studied at the School of Art, Tasmanian College of Advanced Education in Hobart. From 1979 she trained and worked for several years as a silversmith/jeweller and during this time was employed as a designer for a jewellery manufacturing company in Hobart. In 1986 she moved to Melbourne where she was employed by the Victorian Aboriginal Legal Service as Graphic Artist/Consumer Education Officer.

Karen has participated in numerous exhibitions including "Aboriginal Australian Views in Print and Poster", Print Council of Australia (Touring Exhibition); "A Koori Perspective," Artspace Sydney; "Aboriginal Art — The Continuing Tradition", Australian National Gallery, Canberra; "A Myriad of Dreaming", Westpac Gallery, Melbourne and "Balance 1990", Queensland Art Gallery.

In 1989 she received a Professional Development Grant from the Aboriginal Arts Board. Her work is represented in various public and private collections including the Australian National Gallery, National Gallery of Victoria, Queensland Art Gallery, Department of Aboriginal Affairs, Reserve Bank of Australia and The Robert Holmes à Court Collection.

Karen currently lives in Melbourne with her teenage son and is a full-time artist working in both painting and printmaking mediums.

Most of my childhood was spent in Dover which is a small town on the south-east coast of Tasmania. I completed my high school education in Hobart where I later lived and worked. My son Daniel was born in 1974, so much of my time in the following years revolved around being a mother. In 1977 I attended the art school in Hobart for a while, unfortunately I didn't complete the course due to my marriage break-up. I spent the next four years or so working in the jewellery trade as a silversmith and designer. Later I worked on and off as a freelance graphic artist. I left Tasmania and came to live in Melbourne in 1986.

I first became aware of my Aboriginal heritage on my father's side of the family when I was around twelve or thirteen. My mother's was a much more recent discovery. I remember, at the time, being extremely proud that I was descended from the original inhabitants of this country. I felt it somehow made me more entitled to call myself Australian. Coming from a background which had never been exposed to racial discrimination I suppose my response could have been quite different to, say, someone born

Left: 'Hot Fitzroy night'. Above: 'Wobble'.

in Western Australia or Queensland, although I know that wasn't the case for my grandmother's generation.

The response towards Tasmanian Koories is quite different. To begin with: there's considerably more guilt for, as they see it, the act of genocide committed by their ancestors. For the most part we're not really perceived as Aboriginal people, we're merely seen as descendants of an extinct race.

To a certain extent I must have seen myself in the same way. I called myself Koorie, but at the same time I didn't feel as though I was really entitled to. I wasn't black, I'd never experienced the same sort of discrimination and racial prejudice and I felt quite guilty about that. It took quite a while before I actually came to realise, I really was accepted by the community. Eventually I began to understand what being Koorie was. It's something that's not determined by the colour of your skin. It's a spiritual link, with the land, with the people. It's your birthright.

My involvement in art really began in 1987 through the "Aboriginal Australian Views in Print and Poster" exhibition. Prior to that, I'd done very little other than graphic art and a few political posters. The response from that gave me enough incentive to make a full time career of it. My first exposure as an artist was as an "Urban Aboriginal Artist". I've seen a lot of benefits from that. It certainly opened a few doors. It's a good thing that Aboriginal art, in particular the less traditional art, is now receiving the recognition it deserves. The label, "Aboriginal Artist" concerns me though, partly because we're being pigeon-holed and partly because I don't want to see myself as having any unfair advantage over other artists due to all the attention we're now receiving. To be an artist in any environment requires a pretty strong commitment. Most of the artists I know have that, whether they're Koorie or not. I'm an artist who happens to be Aboriginal, not an "Aboriginal Artist". I don't feel I have to prove I'm a Koorie but I do have to prove to myself that I'm an artist in my own right and that my work can stand on it's own merit. I believe that's particularly important for all of us: that we are eventually accepted into the mainstream of contemporary Australian art.

My work draws a lot of inspiration from early rock art but my influences are fairly diverse. Stylistically it's probably more derivative of the expressionists. I see my art as an emotional release. Sexual politics is often a recurrent theme — this is fairly evident — but there's usually an underlying environmental message there as well. My figurative images are symbolic representations of the earth: the land and it's spirit. There, incongruity in the urban landscape reflects our alienation and exploitation of the environment.

GORDON BENNETT: *Artist*

After escaping from years of work at Telecom, Gordon Bennett started to paint. Much of Gordon's work is highly formalised, with strong social and political comment. He often uses grids which relates, he says, to the art of the Renaissance and its use of perspective as a way of constructing a harmonious reality. Gordon plays on the notion of false harmony; he uses the construction of receding arches to convey the idea of the construction of a belief system. He often uses mixtures of montage, grids and words in his work. He currently lives and works from his home in Brisbane.

I was born in Monto, north-west of Brisbane. My father was an Englishman, he was working over here with an electrical company. He met my mother at Monto close to where she lived at Cherbourg, where she lived on an Aboriginal mission. We spent four years travelling around, then we went down to Victoria and lived there for eight years. I discovered I was of Aboriginal descent when I was about eleven and I didn't like it very much. The reasons I didn't like it much was because I'd been conditioned by living in white Anglo-Saxon society and I'd learnt about Aboriginals at school. We'd learnt that they were primitive, that they used sticks to dig with and ate grubs. That was about as deep as it went. So I wasn't too keen to let people know that I was Aboriginal. Later in life I'd be at work and hear people telling jokes about Abos and boongs and that really hurt in a way.

I started to put down this feeling of my own Aboriginality, deep down, and I actually started despising it. This of course led to a low self-esteem – something which I didn't have much of to begin with. I had a father who was really into ridicule: his parents had been in India during the Raj period and his father was a Sergeant Major in the British army. Of course there was a big explosion in the family when they found out that he had had a baby to an Aboriginal woman... My father himself was a bit racist (I can't blame my father too much, he was a victim of his conditioning). I can quote him as saying Aborigines are all so ugly even though he married one!

When I was about thirty I wasn't feeling very happy with my life. I'd spent eleven years working at Telecom and was really hating it at this stage. I had been reading a lot, mainly to separate myself from all these boong jokes during lunch time.

My mother too would have had problems with this. *She* grew up in an orphanage not knowing who her father was – some white fella, she was told. She suffered a lot of ridicule at school which she told me about. I guessed she wanted to push this Aboriginality away as well. So it wasn't discussed in our family at all. I guess she really wanted to be white middle class. She had worked a lot with upper middle-class people as a servant. I guess she had these aspirations to be like them, she used to tell me to vote Liberal...

I started to read lots of books on psychology. I always felt very different to the people around me, I was never interested in the things they were interested in. I always felt like an ugly duckling in a way. I went through a process of finding out about myself through courses and through psychotherapy. Doing personal therapy, I found the energy to get out of Telecom. This was quite difficult because by my stage of life you tend to think you can't do anything else — but I wasn't looking forward to thirty more years of slow death... I went to art college and I really felt like I'd come home. I did very well and learnt a lot and I've been a practising artist now for a couple of years.

Not liking what I was, this was my major problem. By going to art college I was coming out saying, I am of Aboriginal descent, *I am Aboriginal.* This was a big step, letting people know. You can't really believe how hard it was to say just those three words, *I am Aboriginal.* It does affect you, people look at you differently. There's always this kind of quietness that descends after you've said them. It was very real.

So that was part of my coming to understand myself: you can't go through life hating a part of yourself. You have to accept it and integrate it and become a more whole person. This is what my project is all about — not only through my art but in my coming to understand for myself that I am a measure of Australia and of Australian culture, that I was conditioned and socialised into this culture in a fairly average way. I feel that by deconstructing my false notions about myself and about my Aboriginality then, in some way, I am also reflecting how that is being falsely reflected within Australian culture. So, there's this connection between my deconstructing this image in myself and deconstructing it in Australian culture.

I was painting in what was always termed an expressionistic style. On one particular painting — one that I found to be a really cathartic experience — I used the words "Abo, Boong, Koon, Darkie, Heathen, Nigger" next to a figure being hung from the roof: this painting was of course about the conditioning process of being categorised by these words. These words have a lot of derogatory associations attached to them. Some people say oh

'The nine ricochets (fall down black fella, jump up white fella)', 1990, oil and acrylic on canvas and canvas board, 220 x 182 cm. Courtesy the collection of Michael Machin.

'Abstraction (of faith and resurrection) no 2', 1990, oil on canvas, each panel 60 x 60 cm, private collection.

it's just a word — but it's always more than just a word. I mean, language is very important... because it's the way we construct our view of the world. Without "just words" you wouldn't have culture, you wouldn't be able to determine the reality around you or determine your place within it. The experience of these particular words, of writing them up there, was very cathartic. So much so that I burst into tears as soon as I'd done them because they started repeating in my head. Then someone suggested I should use more words, so I went from there. I looked at the work of Colin McCahon, a New Zealand painter from around the 1950s. I had a real feeling for some of his paintings, so I did a couple of paintings relating to his *The Valley of Dry Bones*. There's also this question of belief. I started questioning all the beliefs I've had instilled into me through my conditioning process — ideas of progress, ideas of mechanisation and modernism, the idea of commercial profit and short-term gain and generation of wealth...

I only use the basic units of language, only the first three letters of the alphabet: ABC, or, as a coincidence, "Abo, Boong, Coon." I start with these three letters which combine with the other basic units of the alphabet to create a world view; I use these three letters because I also feel they relate to the trinity, which is another basis for Western culture. I guess people invent gods, they invent father-figures so that they feel they are being looked after. But then this feeling of safety is out of their control, someone else is looking after it. I question all these basic fundamental references of Western culture: for instance the belief that God did give us the world to be used and abused, that he gave us language which constructs the world around us, that this is all God-given or natural. It's *not* natural, *none* of it is natural, none of it is the way things are or the way they should be because we always have this ability to construct things and therefore to change them. I think we need a more holistic model of life, a more holistic world-view rather than this one of linear progression.

My work at the moment is concerned more with these ideas. Having almost come to terms with my Aboriginality, I now feel a bit freer to part from that notion of how an Aboriginal person is constructed. That will always be part of my work — but now I think more along the Aboriginal notion of being a part of nature and looking after the land, the notion that by looking after the land we look after ourselves. And now I think that's the only kind of God you need. You look after the world you live in and the diversity of life with which we share it, and you therefore look after yourself... that's probably the meaning of divinity to me.

I'm interested in how meaning can be manipulated by using images, how mythologies are built around the idea of the bush in Western painting.

For instance Hans Heysen romanticised the Australian bushmen and farmers and made them into heroic figures — but these same heroic figures were marauding around the countryside killing off whole tribes of my ancestors and then going to church on Sunday and praying. There's this sort of mythology, and people just *want* to believe it.

That's what we were seeing during the Bicentenary — you know, the idea how fantastic it was that all those pioneers went out there and carved all this new country out of nothing... how they braved the elements and set sail into unknown territory. In fact they came over here and because they saw no buildings and no institutions that were part of their culture and of how they measured culture and landscape etcetera they just decided that right this place is empty! Had they bothered to study the culture that *was* there they would have discovered that it was a highly developed and sophisticated culture, that this culture had developed to the highest level that it could have, given there were no crops, foods or animals available for domesticating for an agricultural society to develop. Agriculture is the basis for European culture, it implies you're static and that you can start collecting information and keeping it in one spot. But the Aboriginal people had to carry their information about the land all around with them, so consequently they had stories and dances to transmit instead...

These notions of Aboriginal culture and of other indigenous cultures around the world as primitive are due to the idea of progress and of modernism. Modernism started in the eighteenth century with the so-called Enlightenment. I think it's time to let go of these old notions of what is primitive and what is sophisticated and have a more balanced vision, a wider vison of what is progress... What I'll be trying to do is to direct my work more along these lines.

Any authentic Australian identity comes from the Aboriginality of its first people. I think that is proven time and time again by the appropriation of, say, boomerangs for use as an Australian insignia. Continually, whenever contemporary Australian culture wants to give itself an authentic Australian identity, it appropriates Aboriginality. So what we really need to do is broaden our consciousness by including Aboriginal studies within schools so that Aboriginality becomes part of the Australian mainstream consciousness of seeing the world, of seeing Australia itself and of interpreting what we see around us.

OODGEROO NOONUCCAL:
Writer, Poet and Educator

Oodgeroo Noonuccal was the first Aboriginal poet to have a book published, We Are Going, *which then went on to become a best-seller. Her work, which gained huge attention, has since been seen as playing an important role in the recognition of citizenship rights for Aboriginals after the 1967 referendum.*

Oodgeroo was Queensland secretary of the Federal Council of the Aboriginal Advancement League and has actively fought for the "Aboriginal Charter of Rights" whose aim is to improve Aboriginal living conditions. In 1970 her third book of poems, My People, *was published; it was followed by* Stradbroke Dreamtime *and then in 1972, by* Father Sky and Mother Earth.

Born in 1920 Oodgeroo spent her early childhood on Stradbroke Island and worked as a domestic, then as a telephonist in the Australian Women's Auxiliary and also as a stenographer.

My name is Oodgeroo, of the tribe Noonuccal, custodian of the land that the white man calls Stradbroke Island and that the Aboriginal people call Minjerribah. Oodgeroo means "paperbark tree". Because I'm a writer I was given that name because I need paperbark and charcoal, you see. So my responsibility to the paperbark tree is to respect it, never to let any one harm it or chop it down. In this way we have instilled in us wonderful conservation methods!

I went to live in Brisbane while my kids were at school and I've been back here on the Island since 1970. We lived up the road here, with my mum and dad. My father wasn't under the Act because his father was a white man, you can't put a white man under the Act. When my father fell in love with my mother, who was under the Act, he immediately said. "I want her out of this Act." And he got her out. You can't have a man not under the Act and have his wife under it, so my mother was released when she married my father.

When I came back I wanted to set up a museum and art gallery here but the Government didn't help me and eventually I thought, "My God, while I'm waiting for that why don't I just open the place up to teach the children?" And in they flocked... Me and my big mouth!

I disagree with social workers when they say mothers need a holiday away from their children. What I think is that mothers need a holiday away

NOT MY STYLE

Not my style?
Man! the world will end
And you complain.
I want to do
The things I have not done.
Not just taste the nectar of Gods
But drown in it too.
Shed my grass-root skin.
Emerge!
As woman!
    poet!
        writer!
            musician!

Eat herbs;
Chew grass;
Commit suicide;
Live.
Stuff myself
Of the bitter and the sweet,
Before,
    that thing,
        that thing,
            outside
Comes.

— **OODGEROO NOONUCCAL**

from the *responsibility* of their children; and this place is perfect for that. I have a rotunda, built for me by the Shannon people from Nimbin, and I teach the children in there. I've had about 28 000 kids through here since 1970. It's the children who will rewrite history, not the adults. The adults are mentally constipated, children are wide open. I insist, when the children come, that some parents and teachers come with them. It's no good talking to children unless parents and teachers are with them, *they* need more education than children...

I talk to all children, colour doesn't mean a damn thing to me. There's too much black and too much white. I'm getting sick to death of this black-and-white syndrome, it seems to be cropping up all the time. I've talked to a fair proportion of Aboriginal *and* a fair proportion of white children and I lecture them *both* on the culture of the Aboriginal people, on black writers as well as white writers, on the balance of nature, on conservation, on how to treat every living thing as a brother or sister, and on how every living thing was created by the rainbow serpent and must be respected for that reason. That's the main thing: the balance of nature.

Some little children come in and say "But God made the world." And I say "Yes, according to your religion, yes, God did; but according to my spiritual beliefs my rainbow serpent made these things." So we don't have any arguments over that either; they understand: religion is their way, spiritualism is our way. They understand.

I teach using Aboriginal methods. First of all you send them all out to have their swim, get that over and done with. By 5 o'clock all they want is a bellyful of food and their ears are wide open. They're got nothing else to think of, they don't think "Oh, I wish I was out swimming." That's all behind them. It's during that time that I lecture them. What goes in then stays in. This is the way Aboriginal people taught their children. So the children here learn to respect nature as well as Aboriginal culture.

At school we were told everything black was awful and we must go to the white world because the white way was the right way. We were flogged at school for talking our own language, it was pagan. We had to speak the King's English and our grannies were told they'd be punished if they taught us our language. My son said, not so long ago when he was here, "Mum, tell the children the truth, don't evade the truth." So I told the children. "Look, my son says I must tell you the truth, he says that I'm being very wrong not telling you the truth about what happened with the Aboriginal people. They used to play games, they used to use small kids and they used to bury them in the sand up to their neck and they used to use their hobnailed boots and the first one to knock a head off an Aboriginal child won the trophy. They shot babies out of mother's hands, they raped mothers, took the penis and the testicles off the men and made them run up the street and shot them in the back. In the Mildura area 80 per cent of the Aboriginals were wiped out that way..."

I feel all this has to come out. I was accused of being bitter — and that's right, I *was* bitter. How dare this white race who stole my land have the cheek to say they're the superior race? They who pinched my land without paying for it, how dare they? Yes, I *was* bitter and I *was* angry. They'd all say, "Oh Kath Walker is very bitter." But I'm not bitter any more; I *was* in those days, I had *every* reason to be bitter.

I used to love books. I used to work as a domestic for two shillings a week because they said we hadn't got any brains to do anything else or go any further than domestic or farmhand work — but I had tremendous love for books. I used to get my work done and then spend all my time in the libraries. At school I always used to make up rhymes and things like that 'cause I loved playing with words, they fascinated me. I had no intention of putting them into book form until one day I was invited to Frank Harvey's book launch and they asked me did I do any writing? I said, "Yes, I do some poetry." They said, "Would you like to read some out?" And I did. This man came up to me after and said have you written many poems? I said, "I don't know, I suppose abourt thirty." He said, "Would you be so kind as to send them to me?" He gave me his address, I went home, forgot all about it, lost his address but he was a very persistent old man. He found out where I lived and he wrote to me and so, more or less to get him out of my hair, I sent the poems. He amazed me by writing back and saying these are good enough to be in manuscript form.

The next thing I remember was when we were getting people to sign the petition to get the referendum in front of the public. I was in Sydney and had a day off and I said I'd like to meet Dame Mary Gilmore. I always admired her so much and her poetry. She was ninety-four then and when I walked in the door she said, "Come girl, sit" and she handed me my poems. I said, "Where did you get these from?" She said, "James Devaney sent them to me." Then she sent word back to James Devaney to put them into book form and to make sure that it was done properly. She said to me, "Girl, these poems are not yours, they belong to the world, you're merely the tool that wrote them down, they belong to the world, not you." That made sense to me. I hadn't thought they were good enough to be put into book form, it made me feel very thrilled. I came back to Brisbane for the referendum and I was doing the Queensland tour on the petition when news came through when I was in Rockhampton that she died a fortnight after seeing me — so

I met her just in time, lovely thrill, to have seen her and heard her, that was lovely.

What happened then was that Jacaranda Press... well, the manager there believed in going to the unknown poets and publishing unknown stuff (they got a heck of a lot of good stuff by doing that) and so they said they'd run with my poetry but to cover themselves they asked for a Commonwealth Literary Fund grant in case it was a flop. It wasn't a flop, it was a sell-out in three days! And then it went into seven editions after that many months. I'm the highest-selling poet in Australia — not the *best* poet in Australia but the *highest-selling* poet in Australia...

Now my poetry has been translated into Malaysian, into Japanese and Mandarin. I think poetry is very important, it's a universal language. In some places that's not so. The American Indians for example are better at prose. Take Chief Seattle's wonderful speech to Washington when the whites wanted to buy the land. "How can you buy the stars, the moon and the sky, how can you buy the wind?" he asked. That goes down in history as the greatest of all written stuff, I've never found anyone to match him, not even Shakespeare. But poetry *does* speak widely; a friend of mine, a young student, had to go to Canada and meet up with a lot of Indians. He took my book with him, only one copy... and they copied all my poems out!

Things are changing now, children are growing up with our books in their libraries, that will bring on a big change. I think the real big change, however, does not come from us writing poems; it comes through the arts certainly; but mainly it comes through live theatre. Our playwrights are writing some fantastic plays; they're putting it on for the whole world...

BOB MAZA: *Playwright, Actor and Director*

Bob Maza was born in 1939 on Palm Island, a Murri Reserve in Queensland. He worked as a store clerk until he became involved in the National Black Theatre in Sydney in 1972. He now works as an actor, director, playwright and as a consultant in theatre, radio, film and television. He was one of the original members of the Black Theatre group with the production of Basically Black.

Bob's film appearances include Women In the Sun, Fringedwellers *and* The Chant of Jimmy Blacksmith. *His theatre credits include* Are You Now or Have You Ever Been, Bullies House *and* Clouds — *all at the Nimrod Theatre in Sydney. His own plays include* Tiddalik, Rain For Christmas, Mereki *and* The Keepers *which premiered at the Adelaide Fringe Festival in 1988.*

Bob directed Roger Bennett's Up The Ladder *which premiered at the Adelaide Fringe Festival in 1990. He is now very involved with the production of radio theatre. One recent radio show,* Bakeliters, *has been particularly successful. Bob currently lives in Sydney.*

I was born on Palm Island which is an Aboriginal reserve outside of Townsville. My family moved backwards and forwards through my early childhood, backwards and forwards from the mainland. I went to primary school and then to high school in Cairns. I did some clerical work in my early days and then left home and started travelling around Australia doing all sorts of labouring jobs. Then I sat for a clerical exam in Darwin. I liked the idea of working in an office again, doing jobs which required a bit of education. In those days I was one of the few blackfellas to have a secondary education. It was rare in those days to have blackfellas go that far. I remember it was very lonely for me, I was always surrounded by whitefellas.

There'd been a strike on Palm Island in the 1920s which resulted in the arrest and jailing of a lot of people who'd been striking to bring about self-government and better conditions, (my dad was involved in that strike, I remember his telling us) so a lot of people suffered and a lot of the leaders were sent away from the island, I think that set Palm Island back a long way. Because of that we urban Aboriginals used to look on Aboriginal culture as being "over there" — just like we considered the white culture as

being "over there" — and we were in a sort of no man's land. We knew that we weren't really part of traditional Aboriginal culture. We were *told* that we were part of that culture but in ourselves there was always the feeling that we weren't really. We couldn't talk the language, we couldn't hack too much of the tucker. . .

I remember my first feed of goanna. I went down to the shop and bought six meat pies to fill up on this meagre food we had in the bush! I'm sorry now because I've since got a greater appreciation of indigenous foods. My abhorrence for witchetty grubs and snakes and things like that at that time probably came from the attitudes of the white people and the effect that had on me. They thought it was terrible — so I would have thought it was terrible too.

What I saw of my own culture was that it was very supressed. It would come out very strongly only when everyone was relaxed; that was very sad. My father was very traditional, but he only became traditional when he felt relaxed and was among his own — he'd dress and put on his costume and start doing his dances and it would all come out.

I used to find that funny in my youth but now I find it a bit sad that he had to have a few beers before he felt he was a man and that he could exhibit his culture with pride. I suppose what has influenced me most is the thinking of people like Malcolm X. He must be one of the most influential people who started me thinking in terms of the political arena, because prior to that my political arena was to be just on the street, fighting. I think reading people like Malcolm X helped me put black people into perspective in a white-dominated world. Malcolm X taught me how black people could walk tall and with pride in a land like this.

Then I met a lot of traditional people. Yirrawalla was one great man I met: he was a very famous Aboriginal artist. His paintings are very expensive now but when I met him in Darwin I was just a young bloke travelling around. I sat with him for many many hours, talking about philosophical things — about Aboriginal people in this land and how he was himself. He reminded me of a Zen master, he always used to answer my question with a question of his own which made me keep on thinking. People like Yirrawalla have greatly influenced me. I've been influenced by all sorts of courageous people throughout history.

We started theatre here in 1969 at the time I'd been doing a bit of entertainment around Melbourne. Jack Charles wanted to start a black theatre company. Up to that point I'd had very little to do with theatre and theatre had very little to do with me. There was very little in it that had much significance for black people. When we started I hadn't mixed with Aboriginal people in Victoria much. I'd just done my own thing. In 1970 I went to the United States to attend the third Pan-African Conference of African peoples. There I became influenced by the work of indigenous groups like the Chikanos, the black Americans, the Indians. The theatre they were using was a powerful, powerful tool. So I came back and moved to Sydney and did two years with the old Tote Theatre Company.

We formed the National Black Theatre and toured the East Coast and then came back and recorded a production called *Basically Black* for the ABC. It sort of went on from there, I started to read a lot more about theatre and philosophy, religion started to take a bigger place in my life... I didn't necessarily look at what Aboriginal people are doing in white society; what we are all doing on this earth became more important to me.

Black theatre is a natural, spontaneous theatre whose main ingredient is often totally raw talent. Aboriginal theatre for me is theatre for Aboriginal people. If black theatre develops like I'm hoping it will, then it will go back to the true environment of black people. It will go back to the sand with fires all around, back into the open. I think that's how you'll see black theatre in the future.

I'm doing a lot of work with radio theatre: it's cheaper, it's mobile, it can use locally produced material — local stories, local characters and even local people on stage. We did one production in Spanish, we're going to go into Greek communities and Vietnamese communities to teach them that they can use their own theatre and their own radio. We're just a spark that's going to set the cultural fire alight in this country.

The black history of this country so far has been invisible; now it's being written properly. What I think the rewriting is doing is revealing to white people those qualities of Aboriginal society which enabled it to survive the 40 000 years that it did. And of course we're talking about the environment. That's a big lesson for Australia to learn (and black Australia too, I might add). They'd all better start relearning because they've lost a lot of those qualities that that old society had by being environmentally conscious. When I travel through the West of NSW I see a lot of plastic and glass bottles lying all over the place and I feel this is not the society that it was. The most important thing is to provide people with guidelines on how to live in this land — and that's what's got to happen through the arts.

THANCOUPIE: *Potter*

Thancoupie was born in Weipa in the Cape York Peninsula. After spending most of her young life in the area she moved to Sydney and studied pottery at East Sydney Technical College. She is probably known best now for her beautiful cylindrical pots with the ragged, round holes in the top made by tearing the clay away in chunks. The majority of her works are decorated with the designs and markings of traditional patterns from her tribal area.

Thancoupie's work has travelled widely overseas; it covers numerous themes but the central issue is the importance of unity in the world.

Thancoupie's home just outside Cairns lies close to the beach and the sound of the ocean fills her studio. Shelves are lined with pots and maquettes and there's a large kiln in the back garden. Thancoupie continues to work each day and still travels regularly to her birthplace in Weipa.

I was born in Weipa in Cape York in a little village. Thancoupie means flower. Daily activities were the sunrise, and grandmother picking up children and throwing them to the sun, the sun is like a prayer, for the sun to give you strength, for the sun to watch you through the day. My early years were spent learning all about food gathering, about the rain and the sun and how much we were dependent on all the elements, water, fire, earth. Instead of going to preschool I went off early in the morning to collect food with my mother, with my granny, everybody.

I went to a mission school. Weipa was Presbyterian, it's now all Uniting Church. I then went to correspondence school because there was no high school in Weipa, being remote. It was hard to understand why you could never have nice things in the world. The mining company came to Weipa in the late 1950s — it brought many changes: money came in, then the little store became a big store, then you just couldn't buy the four-metre pretty fabric... so instead, all day, there were new jobs cutting down electric poles, keeping the airstrip clean for the planes to land, chopping wood. Now we could buy shoes in the store — not beautiful, not real expensive shoes. Radio came and we could hear Western music; people who worked on the mines were able to afford even a record player. What you just had to do was to try and learn about these new things — things which suddenly put off having more frequent corroborees and going back to the bush...

When I left Weipa there was no major change in my life: I just saw myself as any person in the world that could move out from one environment and

'Mosquito man', coil pot.

Coil pot decorated with animal stories.

into another. I think for years people questioned me about that. "What do you mean, you're out here and you don't live in the bush anymore?" *Of course* I don't live in the bush anymore, I live *here*! I live in a house that I worked hard for, I bought my block of land like everybody else and built the house. I chose to come out from the reserve because compounds are where only black people live. I had to be *me*. I am a part of *this* society. I don't see myself a black woman. I am Thancoupie.

I went down to Sydney. First day, I walked through the grounds of the East Sydney Tech. I passed the ceramics department. I saw it and I said, "But that's what I want, that's what I want to do," so I went in and talked to Mr Rushford, the head of the ceramics department. He said they'd enrol me although of course I had no qualifications. I had nothing except this painting, this bark painting. I just had a feel for clay. Over the years if you just keep on doing pottery you find out more about the clay. I always tell people to take up pottery: apart from anything else it's soothing. It also develops you, it saves you from going crazy. That's why I enjoy firing. When I'm firing, I sit down there at the kiln and I almost think I transform myself. I take myself out of myself and I get into the kiln; and I go and swirl with the flame through the pots, and I sniff... I almost singe myself.

I try not to use glaze on my pots. I use slips and only the colours for body painting which my tribes use. Red was sacred, white was purity, black was death, ochre happy, gay. I went through many years using the eye for a theme. For a long time I was making pots with eyes and people started to ask me why. I told them I was trying to see the beauty of the world through my eyes. Then I worked on dark and light shades and the forms that came from vegetation. Here again I tried to depict the beauty of the forest, of seeds, of seed-pods... Fertility pots are another theme: "love magic pots", we call them, the eggs. People ask me, why the eggs? Well, whether it be legend or scripture from the Bible, whether you learn about Aboriginal creation or creation from the Bible, eggs always form the whole being, the beginning of life. I use my stories for my decoration designs of birds and animals, vegetables, food, water, earth.

I also made tall fire pots. The reason for this is that every year, in traditional law, we would burn the countryside so the yams would grow fatter next year. You burnt the old vine and the old tops so that new ones came up and grew better. So there was a time I did these fire pots which were about telling people what fire is, how it can help nature grow. Last came the round pots. These represent the circle of fire. All through North and South America amongst the indigenous people, all through the Pacific with the volcanoes they have this symbol of the fire as a circle. It's all about warmth, love, unity, tribe and mother and woman.

LES GRIGGS: *Artist*

Les Griggs was born in Melbourne. His people are the Gournditjmara and his mother came from Lake Condan where an Aboriginal mission was established. He was placed in an institution at the age of two and embarked on a twenty-year circuit moving from one institution to another and finally to jail. He started to paint while at Pentridge prison and it was his art which finally led to his release. He has continued to paint from his home in Northcote in Melbourne and is studying at art college. His work uses symbols relating to his experiences of institutions and various social issues which concern him.

Because my mother was Aboriginal I was taken at the age of two under the Assimilation Act. The government at the time had a welfare policy in regard to part Aboriginal children. They were under the impression that they could give us more than our parents had to offer. At the time Aboriginal people didn't have any rights in this country.

I was a real pain in the arse I suppose, I got shifted from institution to institution because I kept taking off all the time. I didn't agree with the institutionalisation. I didn't like it. There were some times that were good, but at the time it's only good because that's all you know. The majority of time it was lousy. I became more aware of people trying to have control of my life when I really hadn't done anything wrong. They move you from institution to institution and don't let your relatives know where you are. After moving a few times, my relatives found it really hard to keep in touch with me.

I've always drawn and sketched. I started painting in prison. I was transferred there. I was in Pentridge prison and I discovered there were all these paints there. Well I grabbed them — I never look a gift horse in the mouth you know. I started playing around with them — I enjoyed it. I just found I could paint. I could paint what I wanted to say, the way I wanted to say it and people liked what I was doing.

Painting helped get rid of the anger and resentment that I had inside me. It was a way to open a valve and release it without getting violent. I got really violent growing up and I got bored with that.

My images have developed. The more I pushed myself, the more I found different areas I could branch off into that better helped me describe myself to other people.

I paint basically about modern social issues. Institutionalisation I see

'Epitaph to a friend (Bobby Pepper)'.

'Nightime dreaming'.

as the most important one, and once Aboriginal people get out of the institution mode then we'll be a bit further down the track.

They let me out early to paint a mural about Aboriginal politics and land rights. They let me out for a reason — all the other times they let me out I just mucked up again, I either left the State or didn't report in. They let me out to paint basically, and I just kept painting ever since. I suppose what happened was that someone was paying me for something I enjoyed doing rather than paying me for something I didn't enjoy doing, like working in a factory or washing cars, things I never enjoyed doing. It gave me something to do, it gave me a different direction to start fighting from. Rather than using my fists or clubs or guns or anything like that, I found I could fight with a paint brush just as well and just as effectively and hit more people in the eye at the same time.

I went to art college when I got out of prison, but I found they spent a lot of time talking fairy tales there. They'd look at a bit of work, supposedly about history, their history, European history, but it wasn't real. It was a pretty picture and the person who done it might be a pretty famous person in a European art critic's view but to me it was just fairy tales. European artists haven't put enough effort into describing life as it really is.

There's been a huge development in the arts because Aboriginal people can see now that there are other ways they can break through the barriers. In the past it used to be a sport-orientated lifestyle and all that sort of stuff, now we've discovered the art world which we can use to try and educate people who don't go into sport. It's a way for creative Aboriginal people to get through to a spectrum of society that they'd have no way of getting through to otherwise.

Aboriginal art has always been there, it's just never been pushed into the spotlight like it has been for the last ten years. Aboriginal people have always been singing and dancing and drawing and painting, since the day dot, but it has never been recognised for what it was. Contemporary Aboriginal art is just a way for Aboriginal people to express what they've experienced in their lifetimes.

Institutionalisation affected me bad for a while. It's only since my late twenties I started to wake up and get a grip on myself, and that was only through help and assistance from a lot of other people. Otherwise, I'd still be going around the same treadmill I've been running around in for twenty years. A lot of people don't have that assistance, don't have that support once they get out of institutions, so they just keep going back, and in and out, and in and out, and that's when you get things like black deaths in custody. Most of the Koories I was in institutions with are still in institutions or dead of drug overdoses, so I'm one of the fortunate few. But it shouldn't be just me. The opportunity should be there for everybody not just one person.

It's lack of love that leads to it, if you haven't got love you haven't got nothing. You don't recognise it when it puts its hand up and you just deny yourself that for the rest of your life. You're not looking for anything — all you're looking for is to stay alive. In the institutions in the system, every day is just a battle to stay alive, you don't make plans for the rest of your life like people on the outside world because you've got nothing to look ahead to.

Basically Aboriginal people shouldn't be institutionalised. It's too hard for us to adjust and if we do adjust then it's impossible for us to readjust when we get back out in the outside world. That's the message I'm trying to get across to people. You can't lock people away for a crime that's basically something to do with survival. Most people are in institutions because they don't know any better, haven't learned any better and haven't had the opportunity to be shown any better. If through my art I can show people a different way to approach the world, the outside world, the European world, then all's fine and well.

Aboriginal people now have got a bit more self respect, it's beginning to become less and less a bad thing to be an Aboriginal person. Ten, fifteen years ago, people hid themselves or denied themselves. Now that things are happening the way they are, Aboriginal people are starting to stand up and be counted, and the more of us that do stand up to be counted, the more chance we've got of getting what we're after: self-determination and economic independence.

Until we start communicating on a level we can all understand, the shit's going to keep hitting the fan, and people will feel isolated, ostracised and persecuted.

I think it's important for me to communicate with people who have no concept of what that kind of life is about; to try and paint so that they can stand in front of it, and read it, and understand it, and maybe put a bit more thought into what they're doing next time they sit in a jury or next time they start labelling people without knowing the full facts behind the situation.

ACKNOWLEDGEMENTS

Firstly, and most importantly, I wish to thank all those artists who make up the book for their time and patience and for reading and checking the edited manuscripts. I also wish to thank them for permission to reproduce their work and in some cases, providing the work for photographing. I am grateful to Fremantle Arts Centre Press for permission to use excerpts from Sally Morgan's *My Place*, to Jacaranda Press for the excerpts from Oodgeroo Noonuccal's *My People*, to Magabala Books for the excerpt from Glenyse Ward's *Wandering Girl*. I wish to thank Duncan Kentish for providing the illustrations of Peter Skipper's work, David Astrich for providing me with prints by Banduk Marika for photographing, Daphne Williams for making the painting by Pansy Napangati available for photographing, the Bellas Gallery for illustrations of Gordon Bennett's work, Megan and Les Griggs for illustrations of Les Griggs' work and Designer Aboriginals for the illustration of Bronwyn Bancroft's work.

I would also like to thank all those people who provided me with a place to stay and put me in touch with artists as I was travelling around the country. Especially Jane Homewood and Grant O'Donnell, Shirley Elmslie, Tim Rouse, Alistair Livingstone, Ron Carter, Rod Imber, Pauline Brooks and Justin Thompson. I would like to thank Cori Fong at the Birukmarri Gallery in Fremantle for her help and members of Boomalli Aboriginal Artists Co-operative in Chippendale for theirs. Special thanks to Elenie Poulos at Simon & Schuster and Jack Jagtenberg, the art director, for pulling the whole thing together.

Finally I would like to thank my parents, Val and Norman Thompson, and Bo Elmslie for their continual support and encouragement, and David Baxter, a teacher and friend whose enthusiasm and passion for the arts has been a repeated source of inspiration to me.

INDEX

Abbott, Doug, 92-95
Abstraction (of faith and resurrection) no 2, (Bennett), *151*
Bancroft, Bronwyn, 133-37, *135*
Baru, Marna, Ga Buthurmirri (Marika), *87*
Barungin (Davis), 12, 59
Basically black (National Black Theatre), 163
Bennett, Gordon, 147-53
Bicentennial gift poem, A (Narogin), 56
Boomalli Aboriginal Arts Co-operative, 126-27, 136-37
Bostock, Euphemia, 123-37, *124-25*
Bowl (Pauatjimi), *75*
Bran nue dae (Chi), 24, 28-29
Broome Musicians Aboriginal Corporation, 24
CAAMA (Central Australian Aboriginal Media Association), 94
Casey, Karon, 143-46
CASM (Centre for Aboriginal Studies in Music), 111-15
Chi, Jimmy, 24-29, *26*
Coil pot (Thancoupie), *166*
Contemporary painting, 77-81, 90-91, 95, 104, 107-10, 131, 168, 173
Coordah (Walley), 59, 66, 68
Counselling, 83-85, 94
Dance, 118-22
Davis, Jack, 12-17, 35, 38
Day of the dog (Weller), 34, 35
Designer Aboriginals (shop), 133, *135*
Dot painting, 96, 98-99
Dreamers, The (Davis), 12, 59
Epitaph to a friend (Bobby Pepper) (Griggs), *169*
Fabric design, 72-76, 123-25
Family breakdown (Japaljarri), *84*
Father sky and mother earth (Noonuccal), 154
Film, 138, 141, 159
First born, The (Davis), 12
Fish (Onus), *129*
Fringedweller (Bropho), 59
Geia, Delphine, 111-115, *112-13*
Going home (Weller), 34
Gorogo, Danielle, *135*
Griggs, Les, 168-74
Gularubulu (Roe), 31, 59
Guyamanda (Marika), 2
Hollingsworth, Ladonna, *112-13*
Honey spot (Davis), 12
Hot Fitzroy night (Casey), *144-45*
Jalygurr-Aussie animal rhymes (Torres), 52, 61

Japaljarri, Andrew Spencer, 82-85
Jila Japingka I, 1989, (Skipper), *47*
Jila Japingka II, 1987, (Skipper), 44
Johnson, Colin *see* Narogin, Mudrooroo
Kuckles band, 24, 28
Kullark (Davis), 12
Lampost, The (Casey), *117*
Lands, Merrilee, 49-54, *50-51*
Landscape (Abbott), *93*
Lawford, Jose, *26-27*
Lindsay, Geoffrey Gordon, 77-81
Listen to the news (Chi), 28
Long live Sandawara (Narogin), 55, 58
Machine time nightmare (Nickolls), *105*
Magabala Books, 49, 52-53
Mandawuy Yunupingue *see* Yunupingue, Mandawuy
Marawali, 1987 (Skipper), 11, *46*
Marika, Banduk, 86-91
Mayi — some bush fruits of Dampier land (Lands), 52
Maza, Bob, 159-63
Mission life, 19-20, 22, 63
Morgan, Sally, 39-43
Mosquito man (Thancoupie), *165*
Mudrooroo Narogin *see* Narogin, Mudrooroo
Mungie, Billy, *113*
Munjong (Walley), 65, 68
Music, 24, 28-29, 101-03, 111-15
My molecular madness (Bancroft), *135*
My people (Noonuccal), 154
My place (Morgan), 39-43
Napangati, Pansy, 96-99, *97, 98*
Narogin, Mudrooroo, 55-59
Neidje, Bill, *A story about feeling,* 59
Nickolls, Trevor, 104-10
Night sky at Gamerdi (Onus), *130*
Nightime dreaming (Griggs), *172*
Nine ricochets (fall down black fella, jump up white fella), The (Bennett), *150*
No sugar (Davis), 12, 59
Noonuccal, Oodgeroo, 154-58
Not my style (Noonuccal), 155
Nothing I would rather be (Chi), 27
Onus, Lin, 128-32
Oodgeroo Noonuccal *see* Noonuccal, Oodgeroo
Page, Stephen, 118-22, *120-21*
Painted dividers, (Abbott), *93*
Painting,
  contemporary, 77-81, 83-85, 86-91, 92-95, 104-10, 123, 126-27, 128-32, 143-46, 147-53, 168-73

  traditional, 44-48, 96-99
Poetry, 12, 14, 16, 34, 154, 157-58
Pottery, 164-67
Publishing, 49, 52-54
Raparapa (Marshall), 52
Reading the country (Roe), 31
Retrospect (Davis), 14
Roe, Paddy, *1, 30,* 31-33
Shark (Tungutalum), *74*
Skipper, Peter, 44-48, *45*
Songwriting, 28-29 *see also* Music
Sounds of the Nullarbor (Lindsay), *80*
Storm, The (Weller), 37
Story about feeling, A (Neidje), 59
Storytelling, 31-33, 61
Story of crow, The (Torres), 52, 61
Stradbroke Dreamtime (Noonuccal), 154
Sun/Wanarringa design (Tungutalum), *71*
Sunset and shadows (Weller), 38
Syron, Brian, 138-42, *140*
Teaching, 101, 154-56
Thancoupie, 164-67
Theatre, 12, 16-17, 38, 59, 65-69, 138-141, 159, 162-63
Tiwi Designs, 72, 74-76
Torres, Pat, 60-64
Traditional painting, 44-48
Tungutalum, Bede, 72-76
Turtle hunting at Bremer Island (Marika), *89*
Untitled work (Lindsay), *80*
Untitled work (Nickolls), *108*
Urban corroboree (CASM), 111-14
Walker, Kath *see* Noonuccal, Oodgeroo
Walley, Richard, 65-70
Wanamurraganya (Morgan), 39
Wandering girl (Ward), 19, 21, 52
Ward, Glenyse, *18,* 19-23
Water snake story at Pikilli (Napangati), *98*
Weller, Archie, 34-38
We are going (Noonuccal), 154
Wild cat falling (Narogin), 55, 57, 58
Wobble (Casey), *145*
Woods, Pauline Nakamarra, *97*
Wrestling with white spirit (Nickolls), *108-09*
Writing, 23, 34-35, 39, 43, 52-53, 55-59, 62-63
Writing from the fringe (Narogin), 55, 59
Yothu Yindi band, 101-03, *102*
Yunupingue, Mandawuy, 101-103